Praise for *Feng Shui Simply*

*"Feng shui expert Cheryl Grace has created a step-by-step approach to feng shui that is not only an organizational tool for your home but also a way of life. **Feng Shui Simply** is highly recommended to anyone wanting to lead an inspired way of living using the time-proven principles of Feng Shui."*

— Julie Morgenstern, *New York Times* best-selling author of *Organizing from the Inside Out*

"Cheryl Grace offers her insightful feng shui and life-design expertise on creating an optimal life. Her book brings you the wisdom of feng shui and much more."

— Terah Kathryn Collins, best-selling author of *The Western Guide to Feng Shui* and founder of the Western School of Feng Shui

*"Through **Feng Shui Simply**, Cheryl Grace is able to assist us in accessing our highest potential for living an authentic and purposeful life. Her insightful and practical tools provide solid evidence of this transformative work. Cheryl's genuine warmth, humor, and wisdom make her a gifted and inspiring teacher for us all."*

— Peggy Rometo, author of *The Little Book of Big Promises*

*"This 'encyclopedia of empowerment' should be required reading for anyone who wants to permanently improve their relationships, finances, and health. I highly recommend Cheryl Grace's **Feng Shui Simply**!"*

— Darren Weissman, best-selling author and developer of The LifeLine Technique®

"With **Feng Shui Simply**, Cheryl Grace has skyrocketed my appreciation for the ancient art of feng shui and its myriad nuances. This comprehensive guide covers scads more than its title suggests, touching on all areas of energy-based personal growth. Never before has feng shui made so much sense to me, and never before have I understood the full scope of its awesome power over our lives. I immediately put Cheryl's wisdom into practice and the results have been spectacular. I'm thrilled to add this exciting tool to my energetic tool belt!"

— Lisa McCourt, writing coach, joy trainer, and author of *Juicy Joy: 7 Simple Steps to Your Glorious, Gutsy Self*

"Cheryl Grace calls us home to remind us of how profoundly the energy of our surroundings affects us, and how important it is for feng shui to be personalized to fit the unique spirit of the person living in a space. You'll learn so much from this book."

— Jean Haner, author of *The Wisdom of Your Face* and *Your Hidden Symmetry*

FENG SHUI SIMPLY

FENG SHUI SIMPLY

CHANGE YOUR LIFE
FROM THE INSIDE OUT

CHERYL GRACE

INSIGHTS

HAY HOUSE, INC.
Carlsbad, California • New York City
London • Sydney • Johannesburg
Vancouver • Hong Kong • New Delhi

Published and distributed in the United States by: Hay House, Inc.:
www.hayhouse.com® • *Published and distributed in Australia by:*
Hay House Australia Pty. Ltd.: www.hayhouse.com.au • *Published
and distributed in the United Kingdom by:* Hay House UK, Ltd.:
www.hayhouse.co.uk • *Published and distributed in the Republic
of South Africa by:* Hay House SA (Pty), Ltd.: www.hayhouse.co.za
• *Distributed in Canada by:* Raincoast: www.raincoast.com • *Published in India by:* Hay House Publishers India: www.hayhouse.co.in

Cover design: Amy Rose Grigoriou
Interior design: Tricia Breidenthal

Page 168: Image by Dreamstime.com/©Rgbspace

Library of Congress Control Number: 2013930752

Tradepaper ISBN: 978-1-4019-3978-6

16 15 14 13   4 3 2 1
1st edition, May 2013

SUSTAINABLE FORESTRY INITIATIVE

Certified Chain of Custody
Promoting Sustainable Forestry
www.sfiprogram.org
SFI-01268

SFI label applies to the text stock

Printed in the United States of America

To my parents,
Gilbert and Elsie George.
I am
because of my parents' love.

CONTENTS

INTRODUCTION

When the student is ready, the teacher appears.
— BUDDHIST PROVERB

Early one morning in 2001, well before people began to congregate on the beach in Dunedin, Florida, I sat sipping coffee and enjoying the serenity of the ocean. On a weekend getaway with my good friend Connie, I was far from ESPN, where I'd been a corporate executive for the past 12 years. My accomplishments at the network had elevated me to a level of considerable success: high visibility, worldwide travel, a powerful leadership position, and an executive salary with perks. I should have been at the happiest point in my life. Yet I had to admit that I wasn't.

In this rare moment of quiet in the peaceful morning light—no BlackBerry vibrating with messages, no phones ringing off the hook—I began to scrutinize my so-called success. While my work at ESPN was challenging, creative, and often rewarding, I sometimes felt an emptiness I couldn't quite explain. I'd hear news stories of rescue workers who were saving lives when all hope was lost. No one would question whether such a person was making a difference in someone else's life. I would ask myself, *Is it my life's purpose to provide entertaining and relaxing sports programming for the skillful brain surgeon at the end of his day?* In my mind that was, at best, a stretch. Yet society said that I was successful, so I forced myself to persevere. It seemed as if I had no choice: the competitive nature of business had a way of making me feel that no matter what monumental tasks I completed in a day, a week, a month, it was never quite good enough. And if I stopped striving, it meant *I* wasn't good enough. All the while, though, that question was becoming more insistent: *What if the person doing this job so successfully at ESPN is not the person I am meant to be?*

In the morning stillness, I suddenly had an intuitive hit. I said out loud to Connie, "I want to be an interior decorator." Connie, who has known me for 25 years, gently dismissed my declaration as if I'd said, "I want to be an astronaut." But I sensed that I had come to an internal threshold of some kind.

Looking back, I think that I was attracted to decorating because I perceived it as the opposite of the work I was doing—a softer, more evenly paced profession, in contrast to the 24-hour-a-day energy of the network, like the Yin to ESPN's Yang. Whatever the reason, I was ready to cross that threshold. On my trip home, I wandered into the airport bookstore and found myself drawn to a book on the Chinese art of feng shui. I read it cover to cover, and, almost magically, it opened the door I'd been looking for.

Introduction

While still working my 12-hour days at ESPN, I enrolled in the Western School of Feng Shui in Encinitas, California, and became fascinated with all I was learning. As I absorbed every detail and applied it to my home, every aspect of my life began to change for the better. I had an abundance of energy, and enchanted moments seemed to happen all the time. The momentum was invigorating, and I sensed that the question of my life's purpose was on the cusp of being answered. After a year, I decided to leave my thriving corporate career to pursue a greater vision.

I might have been headed for free fall without a parachute, yet I had no fear. A year and a half after that morning on the beach, I relocated to Sarasota to begin a new, happier, and much more authentically successful chapter in my life—as a full-time feng shui practitioner.

Feng Shui from the Inside Out

Feng shui is the ancient Chinese system of design that works with the location and orientation of a home, the placement of furniture, and the use of color, artwork, and accessories to create a harmonious environment. Practiced in China for more than 3,000 years, feng shui has so successfully made the transition to the Western world in the last several decades (especially after President Nixon's famous visit to the People's Republic of China in 1972) that even people who've never cracked a book or consulted a practitioner can be heard talking about which way the bed should face.

Classic feng shui places most of its emphasis on making adjustments to the physical environment to create the free flow of energy. Practitioners work with a map called the *Bagua* that divides a space into zones, or *guas,* that represent various aspects of life—family, health, career—and then they make corrections, or "cures," to enhance each aspect, such as placing coins or crystals in strategic spots. In the course of my formal training at the Western School, I learned all about these principles and practices from the instructors and the books we used—but at the same time, I found myself starting to tap into a deeper sense of the underlying energy that we were working with, and I found different ways to bring about change that are not simply a matter of moving furniture or working with color and images. I found that many of these changes, when based solely on the environmental applications of feng shui, do not work. And I realized that for them to fully work, we need also to focus on what I refer to as the inner wisdom of feng shui—we have to see how these cures fit with our personal energy.

For instance, one conventional feng shui cure calls for placing nine coins in a row leading up to your front door as a way to invite prosperity in. I didn't quite get it, but I did it anyway, carefully lining up nine coins on my front step. Then I found myself getting frustrated because the coins were always moving around, especially when people came and went or someone used the leaf blower! Rather than attracting wealth, those coins were draining my energy. What was that going to do to my prosperity? I realized that this cure wasn't likely to work very well for me, so I came up with my own alternative: I framed a travel poster of a place I dreamed of visiting—Bali—and I started a "Bali fund." At the end of each day, if I had a five-dollar bill in my wallet, I put it in the Bali fund. If I didn't have any fives, I didn't put anything in that day. If I had two fives, then I put them both in. Seeing the poster every day created visual energy that resonated with my intention, and the fund did more to improve my financial situation in a practical way than worrying about a neat line of coins on the ground. In ancient China, those coins probably made perfect sense to people as a way to support and enhance prosperity, but in my modern Western home, they no longer did.

While most of the focus of feng shui lies in external changes to the environment, the Chinese term *feng shui* translates into *wind and water,* denoting both the unseen world and the world we can see and touch. Even more than working with the external world, I was excited about working directly with the unseen world, the world of energy, using the tools of intuition and intention—effectively practicing feng shui from the inside out. But it seemed as if most of the books and teachers I encountered, in focusing on conventional cures, were paying a great deal of attention to the water and not very much to the wind! In several of the books I read, I noticed only passing references to the inner work of feng shui, but nothing specific. Eventually I did find one book that went a little further, expanding the treatment of the inner work to a few paragraphs that touched on the feelings, beliefs, and self-perception of the person doing the practice. I became more and more convinced that here was where the real power of feng shui lay.

I was slowly coming to the realization that the ultimate source of vital energy in feng shui resides in a space called harmony. Harmony, located in the middle section of the Yin and Yang symbol and characterized by the asymmetrical line, is a sacred space of *peace* and *tranquillity*. By becoming one with harmony, I discovered that an infinite number of creative ideas and peaceful solutions were available to me when faced with challenging situations or difficult people. In addition, with a flexible attitude, I was better able to utilize my intuitive skills to create powerful intentions designed to reach my full potential. Ultimately, one can't live a positive life with a negative mind-set.

Intrigued and wanting to know more, I wrote to one of my Western School teachers and asked her how I could delve into the inner wisdom of feng shui. To me, that felt like the missing link—the insights, rooted deeply in character and beliefs and behavior, that made the rest of the tools in the feng shui toolbox work. She advised me to read the *I Ching,* the classic text of ancient Chinese wisdom, more than 5,000 years old, and practice it daily. The *I Ching* consists of 64 hexagrams, each with its own distinct meaning, and it works like an oracle: you pose a question, choose a hexagram in answer, and then study its interpretation to gain the insight you need. I had plenty of questions, and as I worked with the *I Ching* every day, I found I was tapping into a flow of intuitive information, almost like channeling. When I learned something, it was as if I had known it all along, and now it was my job to transform and translate the knowledge. I was finding my way toward an understanding of feng shui that took inner wisdom as its starting point. No matter what the question, the *I Ching* guided me to *look within* for the answer. I discovered tidbits of divine wisdom, such as advising me to return to a neutral mind-set for the answer, directing me to meet people or situations halfway as a viable resolution, or instructing me to allow more time for the matter to fully evolve before making a final decision. The result is the book you're holding now.

YOUR LIFE AND YOUR LEGACY

You often hear people say that they wish something or someone would change. Change is an external event, like a light switch turning on and off. The *I Ching* is known as "The Book of Changes," but the wisdom it holds is all about transformation, which happens when truth resonates so strongly on the inside that the outside shifts on its own. As I worked with the *I Ching*, I discovered that feng shui could be a template for that kind of transformation—a way of bringing forth potential from the inside out—in which enhancements in your the environment would serve as a framework to support and reflect inner growth. Taking the traditional Bagua as a starting point, I added the qualities of inner life that I had found to associate with each gua, or life aspect: for Health and Family, it is discernment and forgiveness; for Helpful People and Travel, patience and an open mind. The result is a Bagua map for making the changes you need both in your home and in your life—it's a way to work with the wind and the water. This is not a one-size-fits-all prescription; rather it is a solution as unique to you as your fingerprint.

So many of us ask ourselves the question I was asking on the beach in Dunedin: *What is my life to be used for?* This book offers a fresh perspective on feng shui's ancient wisdom to help you find your own authentic answers—a completely new way to get and keep your life on course by bringing what is most important to you to the forefront. Using the nine fundamental life aspects of feng shui—among them health, wealth, love, and creativity—I've created simple new strategies for successfully meeting life's challenges and activating your fullest potential. The chapters ahead lay out a comprehensive program of inner and outer work that uses the Bagua as a template to manage your life on a day-to-day basis *and* as a map to point you toward your life's true purpose.

In Part I, we'll explore the principles of feng shui and take a closer look at the tools in the toolbox. In Part II, I'll guide you to adopt five "new views" to help move you toward a "new you": you'll lay the groundwork for a mind-set of harmony, which is really a position of power, preparing a space where intuition and intention can do their work. Then I'll outline a set of five steps—including listening deeply, seizing the moment, and graciously receiving what you ask for—to help you reach your life's full potential and shape your lasting legacy. In Part III, you'll work your way through the zones, or guas, of the Bagua, asking questions designed to point you to your personal truth in every area of your life. These chapters include self-inquiry to help you see where you are on your own life journey, along with insight into the inner wisdom of each gua and ways to anchor the wisdom in the physical environment through feng shui décor, intentional design, and placement that maximizes energy flow. By identifying what matters most and removing the old emotional obstacles and limiting beliefs that stand in your way, you'll find you can at last live your life fully and confidently in the face of any challenge.

Let the journey to your full potential begin!

PART I

CHAPTER 1

THE ENERGY OF YOUR LIFE

Take the first step in faith. You don't have to see the whole staircase; just take the first step.

— DR. MARTIN LUTHER KING, JR.

Even if you think you don't know anything about feng shui, you know how you feel when you walk into a room. Sometimes the space just feels right— you like the way it looks, you're relaxed in it, you notice that other people seem relaxed too—and other times, it seems off somehow. You may be able to pinpoint the problem using good old-fashioned common sense: for example, you might observe that a room's furnishings are out of balance with its dimensions or that a building's orientation clashes with the contours of the land, as if the structure had been dropped on that spot against its will. Or you may dismiss your feeling as merely "bad vibes." Either way, what you're responding to is the energy of the space.

Everything in creation is made up of electromagnetic energy fields vibrating at different frequencies. This energy is what the Chinese call *chi* (pronounced "chee"), the vital life force of the Universe. The strength and quality of the chi is articulated in the color, shape, texture, sound, or substance of every object, every person, and every aspect of the world around us. Other cultures express energy in a similar way; the Japanese call it *qi,* and the Hindus call it *prana.* Even Western science is getting onboard, beginning to take a serious look at ancient Chinese medical techniques that focus on chi to maintain health and wellness. In that view, restoring and balancing chi is believed to empower people to achieve things they might not otherwise be capable of.

Vital energy is present in every person, object, and place. This energy has a direct impact on how our physical, emotional, and spiritual bodies feel, and the makeup of any environment determines the level and quality of energy that we can draw upon to live. Therefore, our own vital energy is either supported or depleted by everything in the environment. The goal of feng shui is to improve and elevate the energy around us, which ultimately boosts our own energy to a more awakened state.

In feng shui, the retention or dissipation of energy is believed to affect a person's health, wealth, power, and even luck. Further, the color, shape, and physical location of each item in a space are thought to affect the flow of energy by slowing it down, redirecting it, or accelerating it. In a harmonious living or work environment, energy relies on a comfortable traffic flow, a blend of natural and indoor lighting, good air circulation, and clean, uncluttered, spacious surroundings. Depending on how you arrange your furnishings, you're either helping or blocking the natural circulation of energy. For example, you may have encountered the feng shui concept of "poison arrows"—pointed, angled, or sharp objects, such as the corner of a table or a building, that might be aimed directly at you, your office window, or your front door. Shapes and structures such as these direct a strong, attacking energy toward your personal energy field, so it's best to avoid sleeping, sitting, working, or living in spaces aligned with this invisible cutting force. Just as cement dividers on a highway can create either hazardous roadblocks or useful boundaries to speed the safe flow of traffic, so can objects either diminish or assist the flow of nourishing chi, and thus the quality of life.

ENERGY IN YOUR ENVIRONMENT

We accept readily enough that living things, such as human beings, are composite fields of energy. We can comprehend that a transfer of energy is required to drive our computers and cell phones. And it's reasonable to depict a household plant as living energy, because it relies on food, water, and light to grow; without these vital nutrients, it will die. It may be more of a stretch to envision a motionless kitchen table as being alive in this way and to realize that, once in your possession, this table can become an essential component of your energy capability. Yet quantum physics clearly illustrates how the molecular structure of every inanimate object *is* living energy. That energy is constantly in flux; it's either flowing or stagnant, being concentrated or depleted. Working with energy involves harnessing the flow in such a way that your environment nurtures and strengthens your personal chi.

Early feng shui masters believed that each of us was born with a certain amount of energy and that this available energy could be either depleted or replenished by our surroundings.

Let's look at what this might mean in the course of an ordinary day. Ideally, after a restful and rejuvenating night's sleep, each day would begin with your individual energy bank 100 percent full. Whether you get that rejuvenating sleep depends on several factors, from the time you went to bed, to the comfort of the mattress and the softness of the sheets, to any distractions that kept you from falling asleep or disturbances that broke your rest. Each positive aspect of your night's sleep helps the body to more completely relax, replenish, and repair. Conversely, every negative variable chips away at the amount of energy you could be restoring.

For example, let's say you wake after a fitful night of sleep with a 20 percent deficit from your energy bank. You were too tired to hang up your clothes before you went to bed, so when you wearily scan the room, you see clutter and mayhem surrounding you. Conscious or not, ill feelings rise up and zap your energy level another 10 percent. While cleaning and organizing your bedroom *is* on your to-do list, you fret that there just don't seem to be enough hours in the day to get that task accomplished. Your energy is already down 30 percent, and you haven't even gotten out of bed! After serving breakfast and getting the kids off to school, you rush to get ready for work. You run the garbage out to the garage, catch a glimpse of the ground-to-ceiling disorder, and—poof—another 20 percent of energy escapes. As you begin your workday, 50 percent of your available energy has already been deducted from your account. You're expected to be at your best on the job, and you're running on half empty. At this rate, how long will it take for your health to break down?

I offer this example to help you begin to see how feng shui incorporates not just the physical reality of energy—such as the shape and color of an object or the flow of traffic through a room—but the *visual* energy contained in every aspect of your surroundings. No matter whether it's a vase or a shirt, each item has its own story of how it came into your possession, and you assign meaning to it in the form of memories, associations, or opinions (*I've never liked that ugly painting*). In this way, it comes alive with energy and has a powerful effect on your well-being each time you look at it. For example, a keepsake from a past relationship can either ignite feelings of love or trigger sadness and regret.

In truth, energy reserves can be sapped or strengthened by every aspect of the way we lead our lives: the quality of the food we eat, our exercise regimen, and the ways in which we maintain our health all have a specific role in restoring and maintaining optimal energy levels. All the decisions made in the course of a day have a residual impact, including our interactions with others. Everything around us, and everyone with whom we come in contact, must be a contributing, consistent, and reliable source of uplifting energy. In this way, we're always operating at peak performance and don't have to rely on a perfect night's sleep to restore our energy levels to 100 percent in order to function.

Of course, energy is also determined by the space that contains it—and almost all of us know how unlivable a living space can feel when control gives way to chaos.

THE CLUTTER CRIME SCENE

Everyone has clutter. If purchases and possessions don't have a place to call home, they automatically accumulate on top of counters, on the floor, or in drawers. Clutter is anything you don't really want or need. Or it may just be a result of having too much stuff for the amount of space available. When you fill your home exclusively with essential items that you truly love, less clutter accumulates. Clearing clutter is the first step to creating space. With more space, energy flow improves.

Imagine it's early in the morning and you've just gotten your first cup of coffee. Out of the corner of your eye you spot the stack of old newspapers you've been saving so you can cut out important articles. As you shuffle around the house, you nearly trip over a pile of scrapbooking magazines sitting alongside the photo project you started three months ago as a gift to your children. You make your way into the bedroom, only to be confronted by your unmade bed and a week's worth of clothes scattered all over. An overflow of self-help books on your bedside table threatens to spill onto the floor. Break out the yellow tape: you've just come upon the clutter crime scene. And as we'll shortly see, we're not talking about the neat police, but something much darker and deeper.

Clutter appears in many forms and for many reasons. If you grew up in lean times, you may have learned to stockpile necessities in order to provide for yourself and your family. Hoarding of any kind points to this kind of "what if" mind-set: you're always planning for an unforeseen event, needing to be prepared "just in case." You may believe that having more is somehow better, that material possessions raise your status in the community and perhaps even define who you are. Even a collection of personal treasures or valuable artworks can qualify as clutter if what you accumulate goes well beyond the space you have to display it modestly.

Often clutter simply creeps up on us. Think about moving into that first apartment or first house. The urgency—or just the excitement—of getting those rooms furnished may have driven you to buy things without much thought to their scale, suitability, or relevance to the rest of the home. Perhaps you started out with hand-me-downs or mismatched futons and poster art held over from your college days. Over time, as your taste matures, your appreciation for the past probably deepens as well, so you accumulate an eclectic mix of family heirlooms—furniture, art, books, clothes, and all sorts of miscellaneous stuff. Maybe you add a mate to the mix, with his or her own freight of worldly goods, and before you know it, you've got a full house, whether you want it or not. Just as a drawer can be so stuffed it has no room for one more thing, your home, office, or life can be equally filled to the brim.

Why do we clutter, really? Beyond these practicalities, the root reason is most often fear—something inside that doesn't trust the Universe to provide us with everything we need precisely when we need it. As Karen Kingston, author of *Clear Your Clutter with Feng Shui,* puts it, "The more you can learn to trust that life will take care of you, the more life will take care of you." But most of us have to grow into understanding what that means. Trust is an inner knowing that happiness doesn't depend on owning things and safety doesn't depend on stockpiling goods. When we don't trust that we are safe in the world and don't trust ourselves to deal with the stressful situations that arise every day, we may pack things in around ourselves, using clutter as a barricade—except it's not really keeping danger out, it's keeping us locked in.

The buildup of clutter is a symptom of something deeper—an outward expression of what's really going on inside you, a symbolic behavioral pattern that parallels your life. In this way, the "view" in your home becomes your "view" of the world and your place in it. For example, if you're hoarding possessions you don't really use or require, which is an issue of trust, you'll transfer this behavior to your life by not having faith in your future. Excess clutter in the physical environment correlates with a surplus of mind clutter in the creative environment. The subconscious mind is influenced by its surroundings and ultimately is expressed in everything you do.

INSIDE AND OUT

The feng shui viewpoint can help you to recognize that your surroundings are like a mirror, a direct reflection of who you are. An artistic vase prominently displayed may disclose that you're creative and stylish, while a rocking chair near a window may reveal a need for quiet and reflective time.

Every object carries an unseen message about what kind of person you are—and, at the same time, exerts an unseen influence on what kind of life you lead. If your life is flowing in the direction you want, chances are, your home has a good flow of energy, which probably means that it's uncluttered, clean, and spacious, helping you feel calm, relaxed, and centered. Vibrant, easily flowing energy contributes to new ways of thinking and feeling. If the energy in your home is blocked and stagnant, it's likely your life is too.

If feng shui provides a way to understand the problem, it also points the way to a solution, and as the book goes on, we'll look at the specific tools it offers to balance the energy around you with your own inner energies. For example, in the same way that homes are "childproofed" to prevent little ones from hurting themselves, we can "adultproof" our lives against the poison arrows we create with thoughts, words, and actions. Think of the sharp corner of a coffee table: if your mind-set, attitude, or behavior becomes that extreme, inflexible, and void of compassion, you've inhibited the smooth flow of energy in yet another way.

Mental clutter is like a poison arrow in the mind, and it too takes many forms that interrupt the easy and natural flow of life. Mental clutter includes old beliefs that keep you tethered to the past; lack of openness to new ideas; anxiety about a future over which you have no control; participation in endless dialogues of criticizing and judging, whether others or yourself; obsessive thoughts that rehearse your history and continually reopen old wounds; and old anger that keeps you wasting energy on people in your past.

Clearing clutter, mental or physical, means paring down and lightening your load. The benefits of simplicity outweigh the time and discipline it takes. By letting go of what no longer serves you, you're declaring that you trust you'll be taken care of. You're making room for something new—something better. This can involve anything, from getting rid of belongings you no longer use to letting go of obligations you no longer want to fulfill and goals you no longer want to pursue. Each item removed gives you a little more room to breathe.

Your ability to trust the natural and instinctive unfolding of your life, even when facing the unknown, is key to transforming chaotic situations into opportunities. From this moment on, before you purchase one more household item or make one more commitment or revisit one more old injury, ask yourself, *Will this decision add more clutter—in any form—to my life?* If you pause long enough to answer the question thoughtfully, you may free yourself from a compulsive action as well as open up new space in both your inner and outer environments. In that space, you more clearly see what *is* important and of value—be it a beautiful antique that used to get lost in the shuffle or an area of yourself that you need to develop in order to fulfill your destiny and dreams.

CHAPTER 2

OPENING THE TOOLBOX

*Teachers open the door, but
you must enter by yourself.*

— CHINESE PROVERB

When I first began learning feng shui, I had no trouble accepting the idea that different environments had different kinds of energy. In fact, I'd experienced it directly, and you probably have too. Think about the difference between the relaxation you feel from a massage in a softly lit treatment room and the charge you get from the intensity of the crowd at a concert or ball game.

What was new for me—and may be for you—was the notion that energy could be pinpointed, described, and deliberately manipulated by seemingly simple shifts in one's physical surroundings and mental landscape. How can you make sense of the heaviness you feel in a certain room versus the way conversations flow or the ease with which work gets done in another, and how can you adjust your own reality to your liking? This is where feng shui comes in.

THE POWER TOOLS OF FENG SHUI

Feng shui is an ancient Chinese system of intentional design that works with the location of a home as well as the placement of furniture, artwork, and accessories to establish balance and harmony. Practiced in China for more than 3,000 years, the discipline of feng shui spread to the Western world in the 20th century, though with some modifications, because modern civilization sometimes ran counter to the protocol of Eastern feng shui practitioners. The ancient rules developed in part as a response to the practical challenges of topography: for example, houses in ancient China were traditionally designed to face south so that dust storms off the Gobi Desert wouldn't blow in the front door. China's enemies were also invading from the north, so the southerly direction could be considered doubly auspicious— but those reasons don't necessarily translate to other places and times.

In the modern West, with the freedom to build nearly any kind of structure in nearly any setting, and with a world of technological and design innovations available to them, architects and builders have virtually no limitations on their creativity. And while zoning is always a factor in buying a home or choosing a site for a business, it's a rare builder or buyer who considers the deeper meaning of place according to the principles of feng shui: the significance of the land, the position of the building, and the influences surrounding it. So traditional feng shui practitioners may view some Western buildings as objectionable from the start—and when one feng shui correction creates another feng shui problem, it's small wonder that some strict Eastern practitioners just throw up their hands. For example, if Compass feng shui, which works with the orientation of a space according to the four directions, told you to have your head face north in your master bedroom to improve your health and vitality, you might end up placing the bed against a window or sliding glass doors—a feng shui don't.

Still, for those of us who aren't building houses from scratch—on idyllic sites, no less—the bottom line is that we live where we live, we work where we work, and it is what it is. No matter how flawed a home or office may seem according to traditional principles, feng shui gives you powerful tools to shape its energy into a space where your life can flourish. Each tool adds to your awareness of the vital relationship between your surroundings and the quality of your life, between what is visible in your physical environment and its invisible impact on your feelings, your thoughts, and your view of the world.

So let's take a look inside the toolbox.

Yin-Yang

The classic S-curve of Yin and Yang is a universal symbol for the balancing of extremes. Yin is passive energy; in physical space, it relates to things (such as objects or rooms) that are small, dark, cool, soft, textured, curved, ornate, and horizontal. Yang is active energy; its attributes are represented as large, bright, hot, hard, flat, straight, plain, and vertical. The curved line dividing the two represents the way life naturally evolves—in a back-and-forth rhythm, like the dance of the trees in the wind, allowing the nourishing flow of energy to pace itself, as opposed to rushing straight in one direction. The small black dot of Yin in the white expanse of Yang, and the white dot of Yang on the black field of Yin show that nothing is all Yang or all Yin. The essence of each resides in the other, making them inseparable.

Traditional feng shui wisdom teaches that the Universe is governed by the persistent interplay of these two forces manifesting throughout nature, in human experiences, and within the human body. Everything has both Yin and Yang qualities; their balanced presence is essential to well-being and happiness. Whether the polarities are health and sickness, wealth and poverty, or sociability and solitude, all the opposites we experience can be linked to the temporary dominance of one principle over the other.

The Yin-Yang symbol represents both unity and duality, interconnection and independence. If you imagine the cycle of an ocean wave—building, coming to shore, dispersing onto the beach, and finally retreating to start all over again—this fluctuation between the high and low points of the wave is the seamless transformation of Yang to Yin and back again. The interaction between the two forces gives birth to new things. We see countless examples of this interplay occurring around us all the time— when summer morphs into winter or night becomes day—as well as in value judgments such as good and bad or right and wrong: these are complementary forces, not contrary ones. Just as the night (passive) brings the light of day (active) and winter (passive) brings the spring (active), something that is challenging, chaotic, or unpleasant will reveal itself to be an opportunity. Therefore, we should not view people, situations, or experiences as "bad"—just as a pendulum about to swing the other way, part of the ebb and flow of life. This complicated balance of excess and deficiency creates the neutral or stabilizing force we've come to know as *harmony*.

Yin and Yang can be used to describe both an external setting as well as a personality. In a person, Yang represents someone who is assertive, active, commanding, focused, and fiery, while a Yin personality is aligned with being receptive, yielding, nurturing, and what we might call watery—easygoing, flexible. Someone who describes himself or herself as a thinker has more of a Yin character.

A personality that's balanced between Yin and Yang gives the greatest flexibility of thought and action, so that you draw on the whole spectrum of energies to meet the needs of the moment. Of course, there are times when we do need the extremes. When your child has an injury, it's your Yin qualities of gentleness and care that soothe the hurt. If your house were on fire, you'd want to take command and aggressively deal with the situation—Yang. On the whole, though, when Yin and Yang are balanced in your thoughts, beliefs, behavior, and actions, you're likely to get along better with most people. When you function from a place of harmony, your thoughts, opinions, and emotions are balanced. And when you function from this point of balance—this objective stance—you can access the wisdom you need for making thoughtful choices in the midst of stress and chaos.

Even at the level of the everyday, keeping Yin and Yang in harmony helps to keep the peace around you and within you. I use the Yin-Yang symbol as a reminder to balance my words and actions according to what I'm facing in any environment. If I encounter a feisty sales clerk in a store, I tone down my response to balance the interaction. When another car is vying to pass me, I get out of its way rather than competing with it. When two Yang personalities on the road won't acquiesce, road rage results!

THE FIVE ELEMENTS

The second tool set at our disposal is the Five Elements, which represent everything visible and invisible in the Universe, including our physical bodies. In the classical feng shui view, each of us is composed of the elements of Wood, Fire, Earth, Metal, and Water in unique and varying proportions, and each element represents traits that manifest as particular human behaviors. For example, if you feel overwhelmed or anxious, it means that the Wood element is dominant.

As with Yin and Yang, it is possible to manipulate the energy of the Five Elements. In fact, each of the Five Elements incorporates aspects of Yin and Yang, that primal pairing that forms the underpinnings of the world. When we observe how each of the Five Elements affects our personality and our conduct, we can adjust the physical environment accordingly, strategically redirecting the energy in the environment to restore harmony.

In feng shui, the elements are referred to as the Five Element Cycle, a cycle of life in which one element gives rise to the next in a never-ending pattern of change. Let's look at each of the elements as they pertain to both internal and external spaces.

Wood: The Wood element represents upward growth and progress. A person with Wood in balance is represented as progressive in thought, having a flexible yet upbeat attitude, and displaying an entrepreneurial spirit. When someone has too much of the Wood element present, it manifests as being stressed, impatient, irritated, and overwhelmed. Chronic inactivity or a poor outlook on life would represent a deficiency of the Wood element.

Fire: The Fire element, the most Yang of all the elements, relates to emotions and the expansion of personality. Qualities associated with balanced Fire include being passionate, cheerful, social, enthusiastic, and full of life. Too much of the Fire element may result in behavior verging on the manic: loud, unfocused, critical, and prone to arguments. Too little of the Fire element may show up as being passive, solitary, tired, or fearful of the future.

Metal: The Metal element represents letting go of the need to control every aspect of life, replacing it with acceptance of what is. Focus, structure, logic, creativity, and clarity embody the Metal element. People with Metal in balance have strong ethics and morality and tend to communicate well. Those with a predominance of the Metal element may come across as rigid, overly disciplined, or obsessed with money and the material world. Individuals with too little Metal may appear overly cautious, unfocused, or unable to organize their thoughts.

Water: The Water element is what gives life to the planet—and to us: water makes up over half of the body's weight. Deep and introspective thinking, excitement, and purpose arise from the Water element, which personifies Spirit and the passion of the soul. The restorative qualities of the Water element include trusting the natural flow of life, being connected with one's inner truth, and quiet fortitude. The essence of the Water element is a balance of energetic communication and social interaction with contemplation and meditation. If there's a lack of the Water element, a person may feel lonely, isolated, unenthusiastic about life, and uncertain about his or her purpose. Someone with an overabundance of Water may be indecisive, overly passive, something of a recluse.

Earth: The Earth element relates to the physical body; it's characterized ideally by unwavering peace and tranquillity. To embody the qualities of the Earth element is to be reliable, stable, grounded, and calm, not rushing and not dragging. Too much of the Earth element, though, results in feeling sluggish, lethargic, and off balance or simply suffering from low self-esteem. Too little leaves a person feeling disconnected, ungrounded, and careless.

In the physical environment, when all Five Elements are present in the home, in a room, or on a surface such as a desk, the space is in harmony, and this is when we naturally feel most comfortable and relaxed. In addition, by incorporating the unique and specific energetic qualities of each one deliberately into your environment, you can expand, modify, or restore the energy flow. Their distinctive properties can help transform the energy of your space in ways that will improve your personal concentration, creativity, motivation, intention, instinctual power, and courage.

The Bagua Map

The final tool in your feng shui toolbox is the Bagua map. This is essentially a map that guides your focus in your efforts to make enhancements to the energy of your home—balancing Yin and Yang in the living room, reducing the preponderance of Metal in the bedroom. It shows exactly where to make corrections and changes to improve all the aspects of your life, from wealth to health to relationships.

The Bagua map is the ancients' powerful template correlating important aspects of your life with various parts of a space and identifying energetic patterns in each area. You can superimpose this template over a piece of land, your house or apartment, or your office or business location, as well as an individual room or even a surface such as a desk.

The Bagua map is shaped like a tic-tac-toe board, with three columns and three rows, divided into nine guas, or zones. Eight guas revolve around the ninth or center gua, and each represents a different life aspect—as well as a life lesson you may need to learn in order to achieve balance. Each contains energy that resonates directly with what's going on for you in that area.

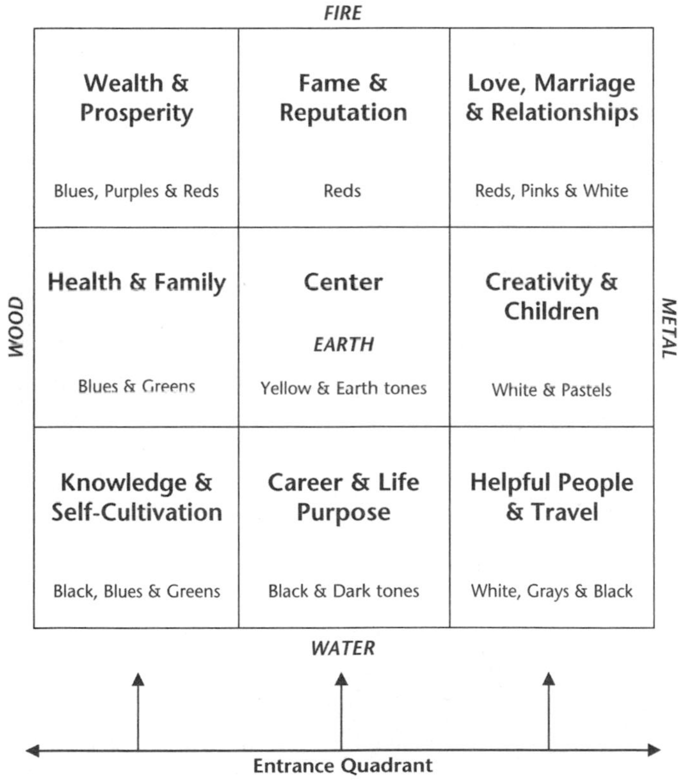
FIRE
Wealth & Prosperity
Blues, Purples & Reds
Fame & Reputation
Reds
Love, Marriage & Relationships
Reds, Pinks & White
WOOD
Health & Family
Blues & Greens
Center
EARTH
Yellow & Earth tones
Creativity & Children
White & Pastels
METAL
Knowledge & Self-Cultivation
Black, Blues & Greens
Career & Life Purpose
Black & Dark tones
Helpful People & Travel
White, Grays & Black
WATER
Entrance Quadrant

The zones of the Bagua map correlate with the energetic qualities we've already looked at in this chapter. The back of a home, building, or property is

Yin, and in the front, Yang comes to the fore. Wood lives on the left side of the grid, Fire across the top, Metal on the right side, and Water on the bottom, with Earth grounding it all in the center. Further, each gua has an association with specific colors, shapes, symbols, and concepts that can be applied to that area to improve and empower the life aspect it represents. By deploying these characteristics in your physical space, you're bringing its energy into balance with the natural flow of life. This energy is at work in your life, no matter where you find yourself—you could live in the wilderness and still practice feng shui! However, since you probably don't live in the wilderness, you'll be working with the Bagua as it applies to your actual dwelling place.

What follows here is a quick overview of the nine guas; later in the book, I'll explain how to work with each one in greater depth.

Wealth and Prosperity: The left rear corner of your home (in relation to your front door) is the power corner for attracting and keeping money. If you're living from paycheck to paycheck, this is the area you want to enhance. The life lesson is to be grateful for what you have, count your blessings daily, and pay it forward whenever you can with your time, talent, and money. If you always give, you'll always have.

Fame and Reputation: The middle rear gua of your home represents how you're viewed by others, how you're known within your community of friends, co-workers, and family as well as the wider world. If you're having any problems with being recognized or honored for who you are, it's time to contemplate how you can enhance this area and turn the situation around. This life aspect also serves to remind you to create and fulfill a lasting legacy.

Love, Marriage, and Relationships: The right rear corner of your home holds the space to create loving relationships. Whether you're single or in a committed relationship, the goal is to interact with everyone in your life with an open and compassionate heart. We need the values of mutual respect, loyalty, and trust to attract and keep successful relationships. Enhance this gua to magnetically draw in the sweetness of true love.

Health and Family: In the center row of your home, the left square deals with your physical, mental, emotional, and spiritual health, as well as how family or friends support you during challenging times. Here, we're reminded that setting healthy boundaries strengthens relationships. Truthful and forthright communication is a key component for building connections that you can rely on. Forgiveness frees you from wishing that the past could be changed.

Earth: The center middle square of your home represents being grounded and living in awareness of the present moment. It's conscious living every day, being neither tethered to the past nor obsessed with the future. You're aware of every blessing in your life and grateful for all you have. The center Earth square comes into balance effortlessly when the other eight squares, or life aspects, are in harmony.

Creativity and Children: The right middle square nurtures and supports your creative side, helping you explore what brings you joy. Just as small children find wonderment in everything they do, this gua reminds you that you can restore your natural fascination by creating something original or unique. Find a hobby, a part-time job, or volunteer for something that shows the childlike side of your personality.

Knowledge and Self-Cultivation: This part of your home—the front left corner in relation to the front door—represents how you gather and use wisdom effectively through contemplation, meditation, and rejuvenation. It's important to create quiet time in which new information and new ways of doing things can enter your mind. A calm mind nurtures inner strength and personal growth, so study and meditation can further any desire you may have to improve yourself.

Career and Life Purpose: The front middle square of your home is linked to your career path and life or soul purpose. Whether you're looking for a job, have a job, or are retired, you stay purposefully connected to your life path by tapping into your own unique talent and destiny. Work then becomes play.

Helpful People and Travel: The most spiritual area of your home is the right front corner: it symbolizes your connection to the invisible energy that soulfully guides you through life. While the name of this gua may throw you off, if you think about it, it's not hard to see the connection between spiritual guidance and helpful people on your path. Mentors, special friends and family, and your spiritual beliefs are all means of support in challenging times. Asking for help is the way of feng shui.

Think of the Bagua map as a way to program your dreams and aspirations by applying focused energy throughout your environment through the use of enhancements. These enhancements include practical and comfortable furniture, vibrant and inspirational artwork, and accessories that advance positive thoughts and feelings by the images they display.

HOW TO USE THE TOOLS

Now that you know what the tools of feng shui are, the next step is to learn how to use them to improve your life. Correctly using Yin and Yang, the Five Elements, and the Bagua map in concert with each other will reveal and cultivate your true potential. Creating a living and working environment that is not only beautiful, but inspirational, sets the stage for prosperity to flourish.

When I begin a feng shui consultation with a client, Yin-Yang is the first tool I use to evaluate the space I'm working in. As I walk into a home, then enter each room, I determine whether the room is mostly Yin or mostly Yang. In decorating and design, the height and overall size of a building or a room, along with the furniture and accessories in it, take on either Yin or Yang characteristics or a combination of both: vaulted ceilings and large rooms signal a Yang character, while low ceilings and smaller rooms hint at a more Yin feeling. Within the room, everything from furniture to art to floor coverings has qualities of Yin or Yang, based on the primal opposites of dark and light, soft and hard, textured and plain.

The goal is to create harmony—to have a balance of light and dark, masculine and feminine, soft and hard, ornate and grand, and asymmetrical and straight. A room maintains equilibrium when all the pieces are in scale with the room dimensions. The placement of furniture, artwork, and accessories should consist of similar height, width, depth, and mix of styles to avoid creating a "roller-coaster" effect when glancing around the room.

One technique to balance a room is to alternate Yin and Yang decorating concepts or placement of furniture into a space in a series of steps, working from larger (walls, ceilings, floors) to smaller (sofas, beds, divans) to create a layering effect. Artwork and accessories (the smallest items) would be placed last. For example, if I've identified a bedroom as a Yin room because it has low ceilings and just one small window, the next step I'll suggest is to select a color for either the walls or the floor that has more Yang traits (lighter or brighter hues) to balance the predominately Yin environment. If a living room has a patterned or floral wallpaper or an intricate faux finish on the walls (Yin), whatever's on the floor—whether it's carpeting, tile, or wood—should not add more Yin. Choosing a solid color (Yang) for the carpet, area rug, tile, or floor surface will balance the ornate detail of the walls.

The next thing I look at is the representation of the Five Elements in each room, because these also can interact with each other to correctly balance a space that is out of sync. No matter how beautiful the decoration, if there is too much or too little of one element, a room will feel off.

Most people intuitively know when a room has too much of one particular element. For example, a room dominated by the Wood element would contain hardwood floors, wallpaper with striped or floral patterns, an abundance of real or faux plant accessories, a décor dominated by the color blue or green, and a preponderance of wood furniture (think wooden chairs, coffee tables, end tables, or dining tables without metal, glass, or fabric in the mix). It's just too much of the same element, and your common sense will detect the imbalance. You'll feel lethargic, yet be unable to relax.

As you'll remember, each element has its own energetic patterns. In addition to the literal presence of, say, wood flooring or water pipes, each element is represented in design by specific shapes, colors, materials, and symbolic gestures. The goal is to create balance; however, you may wish to work with the energy of particular elements to bring more of their powers into your life. For example, if you feel ungrounded, you may want to bring more Earth into that area of your home. Here are some ideas for working with the Five Elements:

Wood: To harness the energy of the Wood element, look to decorate with items made out of wood (floors, furniture, decks, paneling); flowers and plants (both live and faux); cotton and rayon; and floral prints and images of landscapes and gardens. The shape associated with Wood is a column; therefore, stripes, beams, and pillars are symbolic of the Wood element. Its associated colors are green and blue.

Fire: Harness the essence of the Fire element in your home by balancing the effects of natural and indoor lighting; using candles and fireplaces; decorating with fur, leather, bone, feathers, and wool; or hanging artwork that depicts people, animals, sunshine, or fire itself. The Fire element is also represented by the shape of a triangle or pyramid and by colors in the red spectrum.

Metal: For the power of the Metal element, include metal objects such as cookware, sculptures, and wrought-iron accents or accessories. Hang art depicting metal or stone structures. And focus on materials such as iron, brass, silver, gold, copper, steel, titanium, natural crystals, gemstones, rocks, stones, granite, flagstone, and marble. Metal's shape is a circle, an oval, or an arch; its associated colors are white and pastels.

Water: To enhance the Water element in your life, include streams, rivers, pools, fountains, or water features in your designs. Use reflective surfaces such as glass, mirrors, or cut crystal or hang artwork depicting water or reflections. The shape of Water is asymmetrical, and its associated colors are black or dark tones—deep colors such as dark brown, black, purple, deep green, or navy blue.

Earth: To benefit from the energy of the Earth element, bring the outdoors inside by creating sand or rock gardens, placing bonsai trees in earthenware, or incorporating colors such as gold, brown, or yellow into the décor. You can also use adobe, brick, tile, and ceramic materials or soil, or hang artwork depicting landscapes of deserts or fields. The Earth element is represented by squares or rectangles and by what we call earth tones, colors from yellow to ocher to brown.

To move into a more specific study of how your environment affects your life, we use the next tool in our tool kit—the Bagua map. To apply the Bagua to a house, an apartment, a building, or any other space, align the bottom edge of the map with the wall where the front door is located. You can do this in your mind's eye, or on paper, with a floor plan of your home. Remember, not very many homes are perfect squares, so you may have to figure out just how to make the Bagua map fit. So let's take a closer look at how to apply the Bagua shape to your space. Start with a floor plan, sketch, or blueprint of your home or business, noting the location of all the rooms and the front door or main entrance. If your dwelling is an irregular shape, extend the lines to form a square or rectangle that does mirror the square shape of the Bagua map. Garages count if they are attached to a house. (If your garage is not attached, you can apply the Bagua map to it as to a separate building.)

Now that you have a square or rectangle, draw two vertical lines and two horizontal lines to form nine equal spaces inside it. You'll see exactly what portion of your home each gua encompasses—which room is in the Wealth and Prosperity area, which gua contains your kitchen, and so on. If a room lies partly in one gua and partly in another—say, flowing from Fame and Reputation to Love, Marriage, and Relationships—simply treat each portion of it accordingly. If your home is more than one story, you can apply the Bagua map to a second floor or a basement just as you do to the main floor. You may find some portions of the Bagua map are outside the structure of your dwelling: for example, an L-shaped home may have a corner gua, such as Love, Marriage, and Relationships, located in the yard or even overlapping with a neighboring building. No worries! There are plenty of creative ways to enhance the "missing" areas with symbolic design gestures.

Once you label each square according to the nine areas of the Bagua map, you have the template for transformation. You can focus your attention more fully on bringing balance to certain aspects of your life.

INSTANT ENERGY

As you move around the Bagua map, working with the energetic tools of Yin, Yang, and the Five Elements, you'll find yourself deploying certain core enhancements—among them color, light, sound, and aspects of nature. The fact is that if you used *only* these key energy enhancers, without also applying the more rigorous principles, you'd still make a difference in your environment. So it makes sense to lay them out here as a sort of short course in practical energy work. You can refer back to this list as you move through the rest of the book and discover where and how you need to enhance the flow of energy in your own life.

Color is one of the swiftest forms of nonverbal communication, as well as an essential part of our lives. It influences the mood, stimulates the mind, and stirs emotion. Some colors make us happy, while others send us into a purple funk. If you understand the relationship between color and energy, you can alter your mood simply by using color effectively in your environment. We spend a great deal of time indoors; therefore, interior colors affect us intensely.

In general, home interiors should be restful and relaxing in order to rejuvenate the spirit.

The red color spectrum expresses passion, excitement, and power. In some instances, it acts as a warning signal, as on exit or stop signs. The Chinese use red to denote prosperity and celebration. Painting the front door red, for example, is symbolic of inviting good fortune into one's home.

When the red is deepened to shades of burgundy, it takes on a more subdued and refined quality, yet remains elegant. Pink hues exemplify the energy and excitement of red yet are a bit more sultry, soft, and feminine. Anytime you want to fire up your reputation or relationships, use the red spectrum to add the spark needed for new beginnings.

Yellow and earth tones emanate warmth and are often used to calm and reduce anxiety in an environment, especially if the color has a creamy or sun-baked hue. Browns have a strong association with down-to-earth durability, protectiveness, and security, as they are strongly connected with the Earth element. To add more sophistication and style, choose browns that are rich, such as espresso, cappuccino, rustic terra-cotta, or cocoa. After all, who doesn't love chocolate?

Blues and greens are constants in our lives. We see them in the plant life, the oceans, and the sky, and we consider them reliable, dependable, and calming. Strong blues speak of authority and credibility, as demonstrated by police uniforms. Greens offer associations with nature, and we think of them as fresh, natural, and healthy. While both blues and greens are frequent choices for creating tranquil environments, using them on a bedroom wall is discouraged, since both are considered "cool" or "awake" colors that may stimulate rather than calm your sleeping environment. Instead, include blue or green as accents in the bedroom.

Neutrals and whites are seen as simple and timeless, yet safe. Many people default to painting their walls white, especially in small rooms, as they think that the light color will make the room seem larger. In fact, the opposite is true: small rooms without windows will look dingy when painted white. Choose an illuminating color— such as anything in the yellow or gold family—which will actually "throw" light from the walls even before you flip on the light switch.

Lighting can instantly bring new energy into your home and improve your mood. Choosing the correct lighting depends on the function of the space and the atmosphere you're trying to create. Reading and writing, for example, call for light of a greater intensity than relaxing in your family room.

There are four types of lighting: general, task, ambient, and natural. General, or downward, lighting is practical lighting needed to illuminate a room when there's an absence of natural light. It includes ceiling globes, track and recessed lighting, pendant lighting, and chandeliers. The overhead, downward direction of such lighting is considered Yang, or strong energy, and is discouraged in feng shui unless you have a dimmer switch to adjust the intensity. Direct lighting also casts harsh downward shadows that make rooms feel lower and smaller. Recessed lighting fixtures, on the other hand, can give the illusion of height, since nothing is suspended from the ceiling.

Task lighting is necessary for reading, working at your desk, and doing projects and hobbies that require skill and focus. The light is projected downward to illuminate the surface you're using. Examples of task lighting are freestanding and table lamps, clamp lights, and wall-mounted lamps. When choosing task lighting, you'll want to correlate the task you're performing to the height of the lamp and color of the housing or shade that covers the lightbulb. White or light-colored triangular lampshades with wide bases will pitch more light. Dark lampshades absorb light and are better suited for mood or accent lighting. The height of the lamp is crucial: in most cases the height of the lamp should be 14 to 16 inches for desk lighting, and up to 20 inches from the surface of a night table to the base of the shade for reading in bed.

Accent lighting is a form of ambient lighting intended to create an atmosphere or to highlight artwork, collections, and accessories such as plants or trees. Accent lighting includes upward-facing fixtures such as torchères and sconces, cove lighting, directional track lighting, spotlights, and kinetic light such as candles or a fireplace.

You can make any room feel cozier and more relaxed by adding ambient lighting as a secondary or background presence. Directing a beam of light toward an object, using three-way bulbs, or installing dimmer switches can alter light to create a tranquil environment. Dimming your light by 10 percent can also double the life of your bulb! Up-lighting can add liveliness to dark corners and make a room feel taller without drawing attention to the ceiling.

Sunlight streaming through windows and glass doors brings natural energy into your home. Keep your windows clean on both sides and open the window treatments daily to allow the sunlight to flow in. If you have a less-than-attractive outdoor view, choose window treatments that hide any eyesores, yet are strategically designed to allow light to enter.

A key component to good lighting is to choose your lightbulbs carefully. While fluorescent light is more economical and long lasting, it can feel hard and unnatural. Incandescent tungsten lighting provides a continuous distribution of warm light similar to sunlight. Full-spectrum lighting is a slightly whiter light and gives the colors in your home a truer, more vibrant hue. For the environmentally conscious, compact fluorescent lightbulbs (CFLs) use a third of the energy, while producing the same amount of light as conventional incandescent lightbulbs.

Sound is another great way to change the energy of an environment. Playing your favorite upbeat music could bring a more upbeat energy; strategically placing pleasant wind chimes near your window could calm you and lift your spirits. Sound can also be used to create a tranquil environment for meditation or reflection.

Mirrors are often called the "aspirin of feng shui." They double the abundance of whatever décor they reflect, and they also represent the Water element. Mirrors can be used to amplify artwork and architecture and to boost the energy in any room. However, they should be avoided in bedrooms, as they represent active Yang energy—"awake" energy—that can disrupt sleeping patterns. A mirror can also redirect energy, and used incorrectly, can push it away: for example, if you walked in your front door and were immediately greeted with a mirror, it would be directing the good energy straight back out the door.

Crystals, which represent the Water element, are also powerful energy enhancers. They can be used as simple sun catchers or in a variety of specific ways: for circulating, slowing down or improving energy, balancing structural defects, or stabilizing areas dominated by the Fire element, such as sun-drenched sliding glass doors. Crystals also embody healing properties, are easily available, and have the power to enhance our physical, emotional, mental, and spiritual lives.

Plants and flowers represent the Wood element and have uplifting and positive energy. Choose plants that have supple and oval or rounded leaves, such as jade or bamboo plants. Avoid spiky or sharp leaves, such as a cactus, as they can be unfriendly! Silk plants can be used in areas where there is limited or no sunshine, but choose them wisely. Silk plants only keep their color and vibrancy for about two years and have to be cleaned often to be dust free. If you live in an area that has a lush landscape, refrain from choosing faux plants that can't compete with your exterior gardens.

Pets are wonderful energy enhancers, adding vibrancy, cheer, and love to a household. Care and attention to your pet is also a selfless act of service. Pets represent the Fire element.

Water features are powerful in that they can produce an active flow of energy and therefore have an immediate connection with money flow. Water that is constantly circulating is Yang energy and should be avoided in bedrooms for quality restful sleeping. Water features are an excellent choice for the entryways of homes and offices, however, as well as for landscaping in the front of a building structure or home.

Natural objects such as seashells, driftwood, rocks, and stones can bring a little bit of nature to your indoor environment and require little or no maintenance. They may hold a particular association with a memorable vacation or a favorite place outdoors. Their natural energy, combined with their unique structure, shape, and color, truly represents the diversity of life.

Artwork and accessories that are meaningful to you can be strategically placed within a room according to the Bagua map to produce uplifting and inspirational feelings. Surrounding yourself with things that you love and that have the ability to embody your inner thoughts and feelings creates a peaceful and caring atmosphere. In their presence, negative images or memories no longer interfere with your ability to preserve a positive point of view, and your home can embody good energy everywhere you look.

Now that you know the tools of feng shui and have a general idea of how to work with the energy in a room, we'll move from external to internal and explore just how to use the principles of feng shui to cultivate your ambition and achieve inner peace, stability, and clarity.

PART II

CHAPTER 3

A MIND-SET OF HARMONY

Every thought we think is creating our future.

— LOUISE L. HAY

After the customary introductions at a social gathering, someone may offer you that classic four-word invitation: "Tell me about yourself." What do you say at such a moment? Do you respond by telling the person what you do for a living? Or do you reveal what you're passionate about and how it's expressed in your life each day?

When you know how your life is to be used, and you're in sync with that purpose, you take an approach to living that's as unique as your fingerprint; you automatically function in a way that is truly you. This allows you to be present in the moment, and people recognize and appreciate your thoughtful composure and tranquillity. They are drawn to the abundant energy and internal light that emanate from the sureness of your heart. If, on the other hand, you're not living up to your full potential, you may find yourself in a mental fog, wondering why you're not happy no matter what you're doing.

Your ability to feel joy may just be hampered temporarily by a broken relationship or an unfulfilled goal, or it may be stunted by a misdirected career or a general lack of purpose. Maybe what you thought was your dream job has been shattered by corporate politics, goals that don't match your own, or the burden of the mundane tasks that accompany your job description. Maybe you're not profoundly dissatisfied with your life, just beginning to feel the stirrings of a desire for a deeper sense of meaning and fulfillment—a desire that's growing greater than the dream of having more money or free time. Or maybe you recognize that your career is on track, you're blessed with a loving family and a boatload of friends who contribute to your active and comfortable life, and yet you still sense something is missing. Whatever the case, if you're asking yourself, *Whatever happened to the enthusiasm, ambition, and passion I once had for life?* then it's time to do something about it.

You can, of course, reluctantly accept that your job or career—or whatever situation is keeping you stifled—just is what it is, and decide to pursue your passion and seek your satisfaction on your own time. However, considering the many hours you spend at work—or at a volunteer job, on a hobby, or with your family—wouldn't it be preferable to find something you feel passionate about that boosts your zest for life?

What does this have to do with feng shui? Everything. Negative thoughts and feelings are a form of clutter—mind clutter—and in feng shui, as you've seen, clutter in any form blocks the energy that can move you onward to a better way of life. We've already touched on how feng shui can help you design a vibrant, purposeful, authentic life (and you'll discover more in Part III)—but to serve as a viable template, the richness of its wisdom requires a blank canvas, just as an artist needs to begin a painting. The inner work of feng shui asks you to suspend old belief systems, clear out skepticism and doubt, and free yourself from fixed opinions and inflexible points of view. In this chapter, I'll show you five new ways of looking at the world that will get you into the frame of mind for finding fulfillment and arriving at a deep, intuitive understanding of who you're destined to be. This mind-set—or what I call a "feng shui point of view"—will create a fertile ground for transformation.

In our Western world, we're so accustomed to speed, from instant messaging to fast food, that we fidget when we have to wait a few seconds for the microwave to beep! Yet growth, whether physical, emotional, or spiritual, takes time. Achieving your true potential is an adventure. You'll have bouts of uncertainty, even if you are pretty sure of your intended destination. Sometimes the greatest risk is not to take a risk, so what's the harm in exploring all that is possible for your life? A deeper self and truer life are waiting for you.

View One—Simplify Your Life: See What Matters Most

In order to create space for positive thinking and positive change, you need to remove the mental clutter that clings to every aspect of your life. When you clear your calendar by saying no to events, engagements, or obligations that aren't right for you—or that you just don't feel like doing—you open up space for new experiences to enter. When you move away from critical people who refuse to support your ideas or acknowledge your feelings, you allow new, more positive people in. When you prioritize your day to focus on the people and activities that matter most to you, you make it easier to keep positive energy activated in those areas. When you keep free time or quiet time for yourself, you make mental space for new thoughts and ideas that otherwise wouldn't have a chance.

Saying no can be difficult for some people, so if you need to, you can mentally reframe the word *no* to mean "not right now" instead of "not ever." This leaves space for a change of heart as your situation evolves. You can set up terms and conditions before accepting invitations and committing to events. For example, if you're invited out to cocktails, appetizers, and dinner with your girlfriends, but you don't feel like investing in a six-hour evening, opt in for appetizers and leave it at that. Wall-to-wall activities and an endless to-do list take up intellectual space that should be available for clear thinking and crucial decision making. By allowing yourself to have more time to think and relax, you are creating space for new ideas to emerge. Within this unencumbered space (also known as neutral or open space) is an opportunity to prioritize what matters the most in your life. Is it your family, your friends, your career, or your life purpose? Or is it geared more toward the material things you want: a new car, new house, or exotic vacation? Directing your day-to-day energy toward those things that matter the most and at the same time bring you the greatest joy will help you achieve them swiftly and purposefully.

There's an old story of a young man and a young woman out on their standard Friday-night date. The woman is sure that this is the night her boyfriend will propose to her. As they sit in the car in front of her house with the motor still running, he is deep in thought, and she is giddy with anticipation, knowing he is taking his time to find just the right words. He, on the other hand, is wondering why his engine sounds like it is about to clunk out. Could it be transmission problems again?

She's growing impatient, thinking his pensive behavior means he's having a change of heart. He's growing more impatient, anticipating that car trouble means he'll end up stranded on his way home. Neither of them speaks a word. Then, suddenly, she flings open the passenger door and bolts into her house. How dare he second-guess their future together? He just sits there, confused by her behavior but more concerned about whether he's going to have to buy a new car.

In this story, we can see the effects of the mental clutter of expectation and catastrophe forecasting. Instead of placing importance on the relationship, they were both engrossed in their own mental clutter.

We are at our ultimate point of strength if we remain neutral, refraining from extreme thoughts or views in either direction and letting go of our mental hang-ups. It is in this neutral place of harmony that we have access to clear thinking and can respond logically and eloquently as the circumstance warrants. With this new access to clarity, too, you can make logical decisions to simplify your life. If every decision or effort you make in the course of a day is not contributing to what matters most, then eliminate those activities, responsibilities, or obligations that are not directly related to your life goals. As I always say, if you want to get to the top of Mount Olympus, every step has to be in that direction.

VIEW TWO—TAKE EVERYTHING THAT HAPPENS TO YOU AS A GIFT

The people, events, situations, and experiences encountered in the course of life are never there by accident. They are connections meant to provide a message, a lesson, or a test that will jolt us into consciousness. When we understand this, we can welcome any event without fear, distress, anger, or blame. An invisible helping hand is moving us along, bringing experiences that strengthen the character and tune the moral compass. It is essential to trust that you are precisely where you are supposed to be at any moment of the day. Whether you received a bouquet of flowers for no particular reason or got a flat tire in the middle of rush-hour traffic, you can learn to view everything that happens to you as a gift.

How could a flat tire possibly be a gift, especially if you're on the way to work or some other place where you're expected to be on time? This kind of thing may seem like it's specially ordained to slow you down, but in fact it happens to all of us. I experienced it not that long ago. I was driving home from my weekly watercolor class when the driver in the next lane signaled to me to roll down my window. "You have a flat tire," said the Good Samaritan. In the past, this would have sent me into a tizzy, filling my mind with thoughts that I was somehow being personally targeted by the Universe. I would have whined "Why me?" and, in my role as victim, told the story to everyone who would listen so they could sympathize and participate in my misery. From my feng shui point of view, though, I knew that this flat tire was somehow a gift. Luckily, traffic was light, and I was able to get everything repaired with very little damage to myself or my car.

The following week, upon leaving the same watercolor class, I was signaled by a passenger in the adjacent lane, warning me I had the makings of a flat tire. Thanks to my previous flat tire, I was familiar with the drill and knew exactly where to go to get a new tire. I even had an open account. And the gift of the recurring lesson was clear: don't park in the parking lot at the art studio—it's full of sharp objects that can puncture your tire! Without this lesson, I could have easily blown a tire when traffic was worse or when I was in an unfamiliar neighborhood. How easy life would be if I paid attention to all the snippets of wisdom nestled in the occurrences of each day.

When bad things happen to good people, it's understandable that they feel victimized. Most people have a clear sense of right and wrong and are taken aback when a situation goes south despite their meticulous attention to detail. When we come in contact with people who not only have an abundant sense of entitlement but also have no problem stepping over us to get what they feel they ought to have, it's shocking. Even if it's something as simple as cutting in front of us in line, it can be difficult to grasp how such rudeness is a gift. Perhaps there's a simple lesson in the situation: some people feel, rightly or wrongly, that their time is more important than yours, and you're being asked to view these less-evolved people with compassion. And when the "bad thing" is a lot worse than a flat tire—say it's the diagnosis of a serious condition or the loss of a loved one—asking why this particular situation is happening *for* the person will give a very different answer than asking why it's happening *to* them.

In all cases, instead of asking, "Why did this happen *to* me?" ask instead, "Why did this happen *for* me?" From this vantage point, you can begin to search for wisdom and understanding. By reframing the situation, shifting from the question that lays blame on someone or something outside you to the question that seeks to expand understanding, you pursue a whole new direction of inquiry. The mind immediately begins to search for the resolution, no matter how daunting the situation, and to accelerate your progress toward a more productive future. With time, you will understand how the event or situation was necessary to bring you forward to a new level of awareness.

VIEW THREE—PRACTICE DEEP APPRECIATION

If you counted every time you thought or said something negative in one day, you'd be astonished. Whether positive or negative, our thought patterns act in the same way as a high-powered magnet; the unconscious mind has no capacity to distinguish one from the other, but simply takes it all in. Dwelling on what you lack in your life will bring you more of the same. If you find yourself waking up in the morning complaining, be assured you will continue to invite less-than-stellar experiences into your routine during the rest of the day.

To reverse this trend, take time out each day to reflect on all that is going well for you. It may be as simple as beginning the day aware that the sun is shining, your telephone is in working order, you have no aches or pains, your pet is excited to see you, and you're about to enjoy a freshly brewed cup of coffee—all before nine o'clock! Acknowledge your wonderful friends, your family, and your home. If you write these "gratitude moments" down on a notepad or in a journal, your thoughts become even more powerful. Before long, you will see that there are simple blessings occurring throughout your day, without your exerting any real effort. Imagine if you took an active role in creating your positive experiences simply by adjusting your attitude in this way.

Feng shui acknowledges that life mimics nature, in a way that is similar to the "dance of the trees." Whenever wind is present, trees sway back and forth, depending on the direction of the breeze. The sway is complementary, with neither direction considered good or bad. Feng shui also accepts that there are times when extremes may occur, such as when wind increases dramatically and the result is a storm of hurricane force. With every turmoil, an opportunity is also presented: even the most challenging times occur not only as a result of life's ebb and flow but also as a chance for us to grow and evolve. If we can appreciate that, we can adapt and survive any test.

View Four—Let Go of the Five-Year Plan

I spent much of my career in the corporate world, and I noticed something that all companies seemed to have in common. Senior executives were always focused on a 5-, 10-, or 15-year plan. Oddly enough, no one had a crystal ball to accompany the drill. Of course, it's necessary to plan ahead to ensure fiscal responsibility and identify areas of potential growth; however, it seemed that a disproportionate amount of the day was focused on how to accomplish future goals. While risk-taking was nominally valued, it was only applauded when the risk succeeded. Any failure could result in demotion, reassignment, or—worse— just being ignored for long periods of time.

In our own lives, too, we tend to focus on the future at the expense of the present. While planning action steps and a time line to reach your goals is important, it is the present moment that guides thoughts and actions at another level, by way of synchronicity: unexpected connections rather than careful plans, sudden leaps rather than deliberate steps. Synchronicity serves as a natural GPS system. Whether the moment connects you with a person, an experience, or a premonition, there is wisdom embedded in it. A sudden, unexplained feeling could be a message that carries a directive or even a warning.

If you're focused only on the future, you'll miss these important moment-to-moment cues that help you stay on track. In spiritual terms, there are no coincidences or twists of fate based on chance. Instead, everything happens according to a divine alignment of people, places, or circumstances coming together in harmony.

Here's one example of how this has played out in my life. As a decorator, I am always searching for furniture and accessories that are designed with good feng shui elements, such as shape, color, and inspiring imagery, to recommend to my clients. I often had difficulty finding exactly what I was looking for—until I had a flash I would define as a synchronicity lightning bolt: *I'll design feng shui furniture!* As a watercolor artist, I was able to draw and paint rudimentary renderings of sofas, end tables, bed frames, and so on, though I lacked the technical knowledge to draw them to scale. I came up with nine designs, the most auspicious number in feng shui, then proceeded to contact a furniture franchise to present my feng shui furniture concepts.

I was somewhat surprised that I managed to secure a meeting in the corporate offices with senior officers of a successful, high-end furniture company. The meeting could not have gone any better! Not only were they impressed with my designs, they felt my timing was impeccable, since they had recently started plans to launch a signature line of furniture. As they indicated they were very interested and would get back to me as soon as they finished their research, I noted that this experience was synchronicity working at top speed.

After several weeks, however, I noticed that my enthusiasm for the possibility of designing furniture full-time was beginning to wane. While I still wanted to pursue the venture, I was hesitant to move away from feng shui consultations and writing to a life in the furniture business. Rather than trying to override my feelings of doubt, I elected to surrender to the process and allow divine timing to take its course. If this opportunity was an integral part of my legacy, then I trusted that the way forward would reveal itself. I understood that these feelings were also examples of synchronicity, making me aware that something could take place in my future that would not be in my highest good.

Every time I followed up with the company, I was told that they were still doing their research. After six months, the flow of communication had dried up. So I simply let it all go. I appreciated the opportunity, and I took the view that if a chance to design feng shui furniture presented itself again, I'd be ready to go with nine amazing designs. As it turned out, the recession was just around the corner, and within two years the furniture company filed for bankruptcy and ultimately went out of business. I understood that had I shelved my desired career path to pursue furniture design, my life path would have taken a backward turn. By trusting the process and following synchronicity's intuitive prompts, I avoided being made vulnerable by the company's fate.

It's conventional thinking to be in "over" drive: overplanning, overthinking, and overanalyzing every aspect of life. Yet this puts us in a powerless position. We become attached to the potential outcome of a situation, and when that doesn't materialize just as we imagined, we feel as if we've failed. Fixed ways of thinking and narrow opinions limit the possibility of new and perhaps better ways of doing things. Try giving yourself a day when you can leave your to-do list to one side without guilt, and see how this allows the time to unfold without structure. It's these unrushed moments that have you less focused on goals and responsibilities and more in the natural flow of the present moment.

With a flexible schedule and an attitude to match— letting go of attempts to control every second and just allowing yourself to be—you widen the possibilities of connecting with a variety of people and events. At least one day a month, leave your home knowing only what the first stop will be. Perhaps there's an activity you've always wanted to experience, a restaurant you've never tried, or a local tourist attraction that has piqued your curiosity. Trust your instincts as the day unfolds, and welcome intuitive taps of wisdom that may guide you to a better job, a new home, a romantic relationship, or a clearer road map of your life.

VIEW FIVE—SERVE OTHERS

We've all heard the phrase "what goes around comes around." Though we tend to think of this saying solely in terms of negative events or experiences—someone's missteps or ill intentions coming back to haunt him or her—it applies to good things too. The circle of prosperity is a continuous process of paying kindness forward. For every selfless act that you do without expectation of a reward, you create space at the other end of the continuum for rewards to enter.

You can sprinkle random acts of kindness on friends, acquaintances, or even strangers to improve the quality of their lives without seeking praise for yourself. Donate your time to an organization or church with a cause or need that brings comfort or healing to others. Tithe—give away 10 percent of your earnings—to help those less fortunate, make a gift to a family in need, or donate your frequent-flier miles to charity. There is always someone less fortunate, no matter what your circumstances—you only have to turn on your TV or computer to see it—and you can always find a way to give your time, talent, or money in service to others who haven't been blessed the way you have.

I recently had computer problems and needed a technician's help. A Mac is my computer of choice, and Sarasota seems to have a scarcity of qualified Mac specialists. After two different technicians had come to my home and I had written several hundred dollars' worth of checks, the issues were still not resolved. I sat down and asked the abundant Universe that I be aligned with a computer specialist who would solve my issues and still leave some money in the bank. Simultaneously, I let go of my frustration and temporarily called off the active search.

A week later, I learned that a friend of mine had been stricken with cancer. As a Reiki master, I immediately began giving her energy healing sessions— naturally, free of charge. In the course of my regular visits, I got to know her husband and found out that he was an independent computer programming specialist for large corporations. When I shared the story of my computer woes, he offered to come over to my house and fix the problem. He knew exactly what to do, and in one day, my issue was solved. He graciously declined reimbursement, as he was so appreciative of my healing work on his wife. Since I did not want to link my Reiki with a reciprocal gesture, I paid him what I could afford—an ideal solution for both of us.

This is a textbook example of attracting abundance through service. In normal circumstances, I might never have connected with my friend's husband. Being blessed with his help and expertise was the natural outcome of my dedication to helping a friend in need.

I try to be conscious of ways I can keep the circle of prosperity moving with positive momentum every day. If I'm out shopping and have to use a parking meter, I deposit the maximum amount allowed. This covers the time I need for my errand and pays it forward for the next person. When I travel from Sarasota to Tampa, Florida, I cross over the Skyway Bridge, where the toll is one dollar per car. I always pay for myself and the car behind me, instructing the toll operator to let the driver know the toll has been paid and to wish him or her a good day. I don't expect to have *my* toll paid one day when I go over the bridge, although that would be a nice surprise. However, when something of the kind does happen—let's say I get a much lower bill than I expect for some service—I immediately understand that those simple donations of toll fees that I've paid forward are coming back to me at a time when I need it. In the meantime, the act immediately brightens three people's days—the toll operator's, the other driver's, and mine—and I imagine that all three of us may share the story throughout the day, inspiring others to give freely and joyfully too.

There are ways to serve others that don't require donating your time, talent, or money. Simply listening intently, compassionately, and without judgment when someone else speaks is an unselfish approach to serving others. Refraining from spreading gossip or from eavesdropping on conversations is a noble form of service. Making a point of not offering an opinion during a conversation unless asked is practicing living in synchronization with your environment—and when you're in sync in the present moment, not dwelling on the past or fantasizing about the future, you're being of service to yourself and to others.

The simple ground rule of service in any form is that if you always give, you'll always have. That's how the circle of prosperity works: giving to others opens a channel for abundance to flow to you. And as you lay the foundations for the inner work of feng shui, giving of yourself, without being focused on yourself, opens up new space for the self you are destined to be.

A New Mind-Set

With these new ways of looking at the world, you will create a foundation for transformation. Seeing the world through the feng shui principles of gratitude, flexibility, synchronicity, and service will allow you to invest in only those people and circumstances that assist you in becoming who you truly are. They will teach you to see what is important to the authentic you, so you can see what you are meant to do in this lifetime. One cannot continue to use the same approach day in and day out and expect a different result. A more enlightened manner can yield a different, yet better outcome.

CHAPTER 4

THE INNER FENG SHUI TOOLBOX

We all die. The goal isn't to live forever, the goal is to create something that will.

— **GRACE FROM CHUCK PALAHNIUK'S** *DIARY*

From the time I was in second grade, I remember my parents planning and saving so I could attend college. As a freshman in high school, I was asked to declare if I was going to follow a "college prep" curriculum. The only alternative was a program of homemaking and auto shop! Though the phrase "life purpose" was never seen or spoken anywhere, I was free to follow my instincts—my parents weren't insisting that I become a doctor or a lawyer—so, as an avid athlete, I selected physical education as my vocation and started on the path to becoming a PE teacher. At the very least, my chosen field was in alignment with what I loved at that time. Even if I had been guided to ask, *What is my life purpose?* or *How will my work be able to contribute to others?* I'm not sure my course of study would have been any different. After all, I now realize, as you grow and evolve over the course of a lifetime, your calling can change more than once as the soul fulfills its desire that you do all you were meant to do.

In my case, choosing to go to college to study physical education was a first step in discovering my true path by listening to my inner voice. Once I got into corporate America, I abandoned that inner voice; I succumbed to society's definition of what a successful person was and the path you had to take to get there. I lost my way until I discovered feng shui.

We all know what it's like to function on autopilot. We get into the car, and suddenly we've arrived at the destination without conscious awareness of how we got there. Continue to do this day after day, and months and even years will seem to fly by, almost as if you aren't participating in your life at all. You simply haven't taken the initiative or the time and responsibility to design the life you deserve. Blaming someone else, or fate, for your misery may seem easier—perhaps even more logical—than taking responsibility for the role that you've played in the experience, but I strongly believe that we do play a role in drawing situations and experiences into our lives. There's no preprogrammed life sentence that must somehow be lived out. Instead, we can create the life we want.

When what you're doing for a living—what you're doing *with your life*—is aligned with your heartfelt passion, work becomes play. Enthusiasm for a particular vocation or the discovery of your own unique talent readily generates the discipline required to make it happen. If you pursue your inspiration, apply your own personal discipline, and set realistic goals, the money will naturally follow over time. These are energetically connected, and what you focus on grows.

In the previous chapter, you learned about new ways of thinking and cultivating a frame of mind that lays the foundation for self-transformation. In the space you've opened up, perhaps you're discovering a desire to pursue a new career, discerning a hidden talent for music or art or cooking, or just getting back in touch with the essential rightness of what you're doing already. Now you're ready to learn the simple steps you can take to bring your purpose into being and craft a lasting legacy. And at every step along the way, you'll rely on a source of wisdom and direction you already carry within you.

Your Inner Guidance System

It's during moments of silence that tidbits of wisdom can enter into your thinking process and not only give you creative ideas to explore but also enable you to download simple solutions to life's challenges. I call these "wisdom whispers," and the expression is a reminder that it can be virtually impossible to hear new ideas when noise engulfs the entire day. It's important to listen to these whispers; however, it takes practice and determination. You have to learn how to hear them and heed them, how to work with the information they are providing.

In the same way that you tune your radio to a specific frequency to hear your favorite station, you can fine-tune life by becoming more attuned to your inner life. This doesn't necessarily mean getting "in touch with your feelings" in the conventional sense; your thoughts and feelings are just a surface benchmark of the way you react to a person or a situation, and while they may be strong, they are not necessarily true. Your gut instinct—your intuition—is the true voice, and it requires discernment to filter through emotions to get to the truth of a situation, where that voice can be heard. That truth resides in the present moment. If you are making decisions today by living in the past or projecting into the future, they're not based on the reality of this moment. Though your past contains important information that can help you discern patterns of behavior and outcomes, and your future should be filled with goals arising from your passion, those are just bookends. Your true feeling in the present moment is your inner guidance system.

Appropriating time in your day for soulful contemplation and introspection allows you to get to the core of how you feel. Once you have that information, tuning in to what is of vital importance, such as health, family, career, and relationships, on a daily basis gives you an opportunity to figure out what is working for you and what isn't. In any situation or challenge, you can ask yourself the following questions as a starting point:

- *Is there anything in the experience I'm currently having that can give me a reason to celebrate?* (Examples: you're assigned to a new department or a toxic relationship has ended.)

- *Is the experience I'm having merely asking me to cope with something that is simply out of my control, like a winter snowstorm or rush-hour traffic?*

- *Is there anything in the experience I'm having—perhaps an opinion or a negative attitude—that I can change?*

Conscious change involves understanding that no matter what the nature of the challenge, you are able to see beyond its superficial limitations. If you're heading in a constructive direction, your emotions send clear signals to validate that for you. And if you feel negative emotions about a situation (not associated with a normal response of sadness or grief from a traumatic event), you've just received a clear signal that you are experiencing what you intuitively don't want.

Emotional understanding brings with it the ability to alter your mind-set so you can work toward your true purpose. Being able to sense that your mood is about to spiral downward gives you the chance to re-direct your thoughts to a more optimistic outlook. By doing so, you summon a more positive viewpoint or outcome. Paying attention to how you feel and deliberately choosing thoughts that make you feel better attracts experiences that are more pleasurable. You tend to attract what you think about most, whether or not you want it! If you're able to ascertain what matters most in your life, you're much more able to make it happen.

Interestingly, the opposite is also true. If you're giving attention to the *absence* of something in your life, you may unknowingly be reinforcing and solidifying the exact opposite of what your heart yearns for. That's why you often hear the phrase "Be careful for what you wish for!" *Dwelling* on the negative sets a low expectation point for yourself and your situation, and, again, is most likely the opposite of what you ultimately want to have happen. Your internal dialogue influences the present and lays the foundation for your future.

Emotions are the signals that will help you figure out how to move forward. Identifying and acknowledging true feelings as the measure of what is authentic for you is essential for designing a life filled with joy, enthusiasm, and achievement. The operative word there is *true*: we have thousands of thoughts a day, possibly tens of thousands. Most of them are about either yesterday or tomorrow, and many—if not most—are negative. By becoming consciously aware of what you're thinking and feeling, then assessing whether it's true and relevant to today, you create a powerful guidance system to get exactly what you want out of life. This gives you the spark that ignites the drive, determination, persistence, and perseverance needed to fulfill your goals, hopes, and dreams.

Now, holding your developing desire in your mind, read the steps you can take to discern its truth and let it grow into reality.

STEP ONE—IDENTIFY WHAT IS IN YOUR HIGHEST GOOD

When you're presented with a new opportunity or meet a potential love interest, your first inclination is to run with it simply because it feels good. But not every occasion that develops in life is automatically the best choice. If your goal is to climb Mount Olympus, every step ought to be moving you in that direction. As we learned in Chapter 3, each connection is a message, a test, or a lesson. Identifying what is in your highest good at this moment requires you to reduce the speed of your initial excitement so discernment can take over. Over time, a balanced viewpoint will emerge in which a clear decision can be made to either move forward or retreat.

One of the best ways to slow down is to carve out time for meditation. Meditation, or contemplation, is not only a way to calm the mind; it's also a way to be truly awake. The purpose of contemplation is to allow oneself to "just be" without external influence or manipulation. Concentration and creative thinking flourish in a relaxed environment. Original thoughts begin to emerge as internal space is cleared, and what looked like utter chaos may also begin to find its own order. This is sacred time, meant only for private thoughts, for the inner voice to speak.

If you're unsure how to create a peaceful environment, live in harmony with loved ones, and find joy in each moment, it's essential to make time in your day for inward reflection or meditation. This doesn't require you to sit in a lotus position with incense burning if that isn't your idea of a comfortable environment. Meditation, at its most basic, is simply the act of listening. It provides quiet time to seek ways in which to live thoughtfully and responsibly. It's a process of internal observation that helps us examine and diminish our preoccupation with self-centered worries.

It's usually easier to take time out of the day for contemplation if you schedule an appointment with yourself, since you know best when there are the fewest distractions. I find it most beneficial to meditate early in the morning when my mind is more alert and clear. Once my day begins, time seems to get away from me. If you are a stay-at-home parent with children, you may need to set the alarm to schedule in your quiet time before the children rise. Begin in small increments—as little as five minutes; as you grow accustomed to the exercise, you can build up to more time. Sit in a comfortable position in the calmest environment you can find, whether it's in an easy chair or on a rock by a stream. Now just listen within and see what comes up. At first your mind will race with all the things you think you should be doing. Hang in there! The benefits of quiet time will be revealed soon enough.

While there are many helpful books on how to meditate, I've found the easiest way to get started is by sitting with my eyes closed, then concentrating on breathing evenly and deeply while I inhale and exhale. I imagine the core of my body as a balloon with no air. As I begin to draw air into the balloon, all sides of my body expand equally. I breathe in for seven counts and hold for one additional count. That moment of holding my breath allows me to experience stillness. As I exhale, I imagine my balloon (my body) shrinking as I blow the air out, either through my nose or mouth, taking seven counts to complete. I repeat the breathing exercise three times. This uncomplicated routine of concentrating on a breathing pattern allows my mind to relax naturally.

I always begin my meditation by acknowledging the many blessings that I already enjoy in each of the nine areas of the Bagua map. By beginning this way, I focus on what's positive, and it immediately lifts my spirits. I'm delighted and grateful that there are so many wonderful experiences and opportunities already happening for me. I also use this time to set intentions, which is a powerful way to channel your focus and draw in opportunities that are aligned with your highest good. Rather than leaving everything to chance, you're taking an active approach toward living your life in association with your soul purpose. This action planning is a positive statement of an outcome you want to experience. It's a clear goal or vision that guides your thoughts, activities, and choices.

You *can* attract what is in alignment with your deepest desires, as long as it is in your highest good: something that helps you and at the same time serves others. Acquiring faster cars, bigger houses, or winning the lottery isn't always in your highest good. We're too focused on the acquisition of material goods and services—to the point of going quite beyond what we really need to sustain ourselves. These acquisitions have become a substitute for honoring deeper yearnings, rather than adding to our well-being. It is important to figure out which things you have a passion for that have value and meaning for you, and that complement or improve your life.

One method to help you identify what is in your highest good is to form a statement of intent or a declaration inviting new things to enter your life. This strong announcement is a kind of universal "shout out" of confidence and certainty that will likely attract what is in your highest good and repel that which is not in alignment with it.

Structure the intention in such a way that you must explore a question about yourself, rather than making a demand for something. In this way, your mind searches for the answer, and the Universe simultaneously works to bring to your attention anything that is blocking you from achieving your goal.

Suppose you want to have a romantic relationship. Here's how a demand and a declaration might sound:

Demand: *I want to meet a rich man who is good-looking and has no baggage. Oh, and make sure he drives a sports car and loves to shower me with gifts.*

Declaration: *I am open to healing and balancing my personality, my behavior, or a mindset that may be preventing me from meeting my romantic partner.*

Making a declaration will guide you first to explore old belief systems or negative dialogues about yourself or others, or to examine how you are perceived in the public eye. This in turn will help you remove any obstacles standing in the way of meeting a mate.

Let's take another example. Say you're seeking a new job and don't really know what kind of work would be more fulfilling than what you are doing now:

Demand: *Can you please give me a new job so I don't have to deal with my annoying co-workers and this boring work routine?*

Declaration: *I am open to discovering what my life is to be dedicated to.*

In this way, you open the doors of opportunity wider in order to explore what you feel passionate about. You may have a particular skill that's gone unused or a part-time hobby that you would love to be doing full-time as a primary source of income, or maybe you'd really love an opportunity to serve others while still being paid for your work. If you are clear about what matters most in terms of what you do for a living but you don't know where or how to proceed, you might phrase your intention this way:

I am open to being connected to any person, place, or experience that will help me achieve my goal.

Then just listen. The answer may come instantly or with a little time. Your role is to be patient and observe.

Another method for getting an answer to a persistent question is to simply pose the question in your mind, on paper, or out loud. In this approach, you are able to use your time wisely and align yourself with the resources you need to successfully meet your goal.

For example, I recently experienced a combination of weight fluctuation and overall fatigue. I generally eat healthily and exercise regularly, but nothing seemed to be working. I didn't want to write it off as due to my being a busy businesswoman or someone riddled with hormone imbalances. I asked the Universe for help by forming a question to get to the core issue of my overall health and well-being:

Can you align me with the correct natural health expert to precisely diagnose my underlying health issue?

Then I listened, and the answer came a few days later. During a routine visit, my doctor of Oriental medicine said she'd been giving a lot of thought to my symptoms and believed that I might have a sensitivity to gluten—perhaps even an allergy. She suggested I omit it from my diet for 30 days to see if I felt better. I took her advice, and it was a turning point for my health. My symptoms disappeared. Simultaneously, I realized I had to step up my overall exercise routine, so I hired a personal trainer and joined a new gym. Though I was initially hesitant about the expense, I made the commitment anyway. Within a day of signing up, I received an unexpected check in the mail for a longtime project that I'd been working on—a positive affirmation that I was not only on the right track but was even being financially supported!

Calming your mind and focusing your intentions will give the Universe a chance to communicate with you through your inner guidance system. It will help you identify your soul purpose—that which is in your highest good—and show you the steps to take to reach your goal.

STEP TWO—ACT "AS IF"

Through the process of questioning and listening, you'll find that you see ever more clearly how the course of your life is unfolding and whether what you want is in your highest good. At this stage, there are a few things you should do before you take action.

While I was writing this book, I took a magical trip to Ecuador, where I hiked in the Amazon with naturalists and native guides, swam with sea lions off the Galápagos, and rediscovered my passion for photography, even though all I had was a little point-and-shoot camera. When I came home, the first thing I wanted to do was go back to Ecuador! I could still practically see and feel the jungle, and I wanted to get the feeling back. It had been much more than a fun trip—it felt as if the experience had served some deeper purpose, connecting me with something profound. In the past, I would probably have planned another trip as soon as I could, booked a ticket and bought a new camera right away. This time, taking the feng shui approach, I asked myself if this desire for a return trip was in my highest good. Well, I couldn't see any reason why it wouldn't be—after all, it's not as if I were dreaming of moving to Ecuador and living the rest of my life in the Amazon. So I went on to the next step, which I recommend to anyone excited about possibilities and eager to rush into a new venture: Take some time first to act "as if"—to pause and imagine yourself in the experience before investing unlimited time and resources. This means being able to play out in your mind how it would feel to be in a particular role or situation. In my case, I needed to imagine I was heading back to the jungle. If you had decided to explore the possibility of being the next president of the United States, you would need to go through a process of feeling as if it were already true—as if it had already happened.

There are three steps to the acting-as-if process: *visualizing, feeling,* and *believing.* The first step is to be able to *visualize* precisely how the experience would play out in real life. In the example of my trip, I imagined myself on the plane, on the trail, on the beach. In the example of becoming president, you'd picture yourself as the president. Is the picture realistic at the most basic level—is being elected even possible (never mind likely)? Are you an American citizen, an eligible age, and willing to devote your life to serving the American public—in public—for years? A goal has to be realistic and achievable for you to sustain the drive to move forward.

The second step is to explore how you would *feel* being in a specific role or situation. You will find the experience either one you welcome or one you dread. Hiking in the Amazon, would I feel exhilarated and inspired as I did the first time? As president, will you feel it is an honor to be of service, no matter what the responsibility, or will you be terrified of having to put in long hours under overwhelming demands at the expense of your personal life? If you can successfully imagine yourself as empowered, excited, and ready for the challenge, you've passed step two. If you're feeling uncertain, anxious, and dismayed by the possibility, perhaps it's time to stop and regroup. Feelings engage all the senses and allow your inner guidance system to make itself heard. This exercise is taking you well beyond a thinking mode and into the heart of your aspiration. If the urge is still there, you are ready for step three.

The third step is to *believe* that your desired outcome can actually come about. I knew I could bring about a trip to South America if I decided to—no problem there. As for becoming president, you may have the initiative and resources to do it, but without your inner knowing and core belief that the presidency is within reach, you will forever fall short in the energy, fortitude, and perseverance required to succeed. Any fear or doubt further dampens the passion. Using positive affirmations to move you toward a more optimistic view of your goal *may* help you, but if you don't firmly believe them, you could be wasting your time.

STEP THREE—SURRENDER TO THE PROCESS

The philosophy of feng shui takes its cues from nature, from what is native to the environment. The beauty of nature's design, whether it's the shape of a leaf or the pattern of a natural habitat, can be seen everywhere in asymmetrical forms. This allows nourishing energy to flow at a slower pace in and around all that exists. If you've ever planted seeds in your garden, you know that if you provide them with water, nutrients, and light over a period of time, eventually plants will appear. We can apply the same principles to the way we manage our lives. When we surrender to the process and let go of the need to be in control, we allow time and space for people, places, events, and experiences to align and move us toward our goals.

Imagine how exhausting and frustrating it would be to actually watch a plant grow from a seed! You instinctively know it would be a waste of your time and not the slightest help to the plant. Once you embrace this concept, you can apply it to any situation where you find yourself anxiously waiting for something to happen. The divine timing of an outcome is not in our control, and when we push for a result due to our lack of understanding or patience, we may even get undesirable consequences. My experience with the furniture design career that didn't get off the ground is just one example of surrender leading to success.

So what do you do while you're practicing patience? You go about your life. You are being asked to trust that help is on the way and that it may take some time for the ideal situation to evolve. Learning trust is one of life's more challenging lessons, and you won't pass the class until you do the work to overcome your fears. Going about your life means following your natural urge to meet interesting people, explore opportunities, and discover new ways of doing things. Patience and optimism will help you see beyond any perceptible limitations. Surrendering to the process doesn't mean that you're just living however you want to live because the outcome is set. It simply means that you can't control the process. You must live your life in a way that strategically plants seeds that in time will blossom in the direction of your life purpose.

As an example: if you're searching for a job in a different industry and you send your résumé to every company in the field whether or not it would be the right fit, you are looking for a quick fix. A thoughtful and thorough search of select companies that best match your qualifications with their need for your skills or services gives you a more focused goal. While tracking the progress of your job search is important, it's also important to trust that the right job in the right industry is lining up for you.

This is the stage I'm in with my idea of traveling back to the Amazon. I have some goals and objectives—to save up for a professional-quality camera, to save for the trip itself, to take Spanish lessons—but I'm not pushing the time line; I'm letting things take their course. My plan will either peter out—perhaps I'll lose interest—or build momentum. I think it's likely to be the latter; already a friend has planned her own trip to Peru a few months from now, and she'll share stories and advice that may help my plans take shape.

STEP FOUR—GRACIOUSLY RECEIVE

There comes a magical time when what you have wished for does indeed come true. It's right in front of you, just as you imagined and prayed for. Now is the time to graciously receive—the time to acknowl-edge that your prayers, intentions, and desires have been answered. You need to believe that you're worthy of this opportunity and deserve to have it.

Not long ago, I had a client begin to manifest her goal to have more money to live on, using my techniques and guidance. She had left her corporate job to pursue her artistic dreams full time as a jewelry designer. As in any new venture, she faced an initial financial investment and start-up costs in developing her signature line of original products, and her savings were being depleted in the process. While investing in her future and taking the leap of faith was important, she still had to meet her monthly living expenses.

As she continued to have faith and trust that the Universe would support her, an unexpected gift came in the form of a small inheritance. Her initial reaction was to push back because this seemed "too easy." Her deeply ingrained values had always dictated that the only way to achieve financial success was to work hard and earn her own money. Even buying a winning lottery ticket would be the wrong way to get money!

So at first, my client was not able to fully embrace the gift as the answer to her prayers. After all, in her mind she hadn't earned it. I reminded her that she'd asked, and been given, the financial support she needed. Now was the time to graciously receive. It would be the same for me if a grateful client offered to pick up the tab for my trip to the jungle—or even if my plans fell into place but I felt I hadn't worked hard enough to "earn" another trip! A true commitment to living in harmony requires you to give and receive in all areas of your life. Being unappreciative or unaccepting of these abundant gifts declares to the Universe that, no matter what you've been given, somehow it's not and never will be enough.

By the same token, graciously receiving means not taking things for granted, whether windfalls or ordinary services. For example, you rely on your phone to work whenever you need to make or receive a call. We question our phone company's standard of excellence when the phone line is dead and we're inconvenienced. But when it's functioning as it should, do we ever think about the extraordinary number of people behind the scenes working daily to keep our phone in service and operating properly?

Step Five—Seize the Moment

Now that you have a wonderful opportunity in front of you and you've graciously accepted its presence in your life, it's time to seize the moment! Here is where you take practical steps to put your dream into motion. As you set priorities, you'll fine-tune your focus and develop a logical set of action items to forward the goal. (It's also important to prioritize the big picture of your life before you take on a new project, so you don't lose sight of what is most important. The big picture priorities in my life are family, friends, and pets; the life work that brings me sustenance and joy; and my legacy, which is my gift to the world.)

As an example, let's imagine that your goal is to change careers and find a job in a new industry. To pursue your new vocation, you'll need a vision that takes in what's necessary to reach your goal—perhaps including financial support, education, job skills and expertise, the availability of jobs, and your own willingness to relocate or take a cut in pay. Your initial action steps might focus on determining whether the field you're considering is the right fit for you:

- Volunteer or take an internship in the new area to gain experience in the industry.

- Research the inner workings of the industry.

- Attend classes to increase your knowledge and gain relevant skills.

- Read industry books and magazines to narrow your focus to a particular area or niche.

- Research potential employers in your area or an area you'd consider moving to.

- Make a list of the pros and cons of the field.

- Conduct informational interviews with key executives or managers in the industry to find out what's out there for you and plan your next steps.

My jungle travel is a different kind of example, since many of the steps required to bring a trip about are obvious and well defined. If I reach this point with my jungle trip—if the process leads it to fruition and I'm able to graciously accept the opportunity—I'll pack my new camera and be ready to seize the moment!

THE ROAD MAP TO THE LIFE YOU WANT

Creating the life you want requires seizing the moment and taking action. There is a dynamic inspirational saying I often use in my own personal life and teaching: "God will guide your footsteps; you have to move your feet."

Achieving a lasting legacy comes from pursuing your passion, believing in yourself, and trusting that what's in your highest good will happen, one magical day at a time. Don't get caught up with the 5-, 10-, and 20-year plans that will keep you from staying in the present moment. Those moments—one after another—evolve into your life plan. Let go of the notion that you have to be overprepared or that you need to have everything in perfect order before you can enjoy it. Just focus on the tasks necessary to get what you want and follow your hunches.

Being who you're intended to be will ultimately result in you making a difference in the world. Confidence comes from knowing what your life work is about. This is where the real work of inner feng shui

begins. You've identified a new mind-set. You've figured out what's in your highest good. And now the
tools of inner feng shui will help you stay on course
and bring what is most important to the forefront
and help you achieve your goals.

CHAPTER 5

A MORE PERSONAL FENG SHUI

*We cannot see our reflection in running water.
It is only in still water that we can see.*

— TAOIST PROVERB

Early practitioners of feng shui aspired to what they viewed as the paradigm of spirituality—a combination of modesty, sincerity, compassion, humility, and forgiveness. Regarded by others as spiritual masters, these practitioners were highly sought after for their insight into ways to achieve an ideal living environment, which was considered an integral component of a person's health and vitality. In other words, from the very beginning, feng shui was consciously used as a guide for fine-tuning one's internal environment.

As I've mentioned, the focus of conventional feng shui books is the external environment. The purpose of the cures we see is to alter the energy of the space in a way that connects directly with what's going on inside us. However, the one-size-fits-all manner that's common today doesn't delve more deeply into the inner life of the person using it, and this can be unproductive—even counterproductive.

The primary goal of feng shui is to return what's most important to you in each area of your life to your consciousness—much as the Bali fund I mentioned in the introduction did for me. Ideally, each object you bring into your surroundings will embody one or more qualities of safety, comfort, vitality, or inspiration. And, as you learn to select individual pieces of furniture, artwork, and accessories for the way they link to your life, you'll benefit by living and working at a more sophisticated level.

Once you know that everything is emblematic, you'll begin to look at every functional or decorative item differently. You'll ponder who gave it to you, where you bought it, what memory it triggers, whether you love it or not, or if the mere sight of it brings you joy. Some items may take on greater significance just by their capacity to inspire. In this way, your environment is not only a declaration of who you are at any given moment; it has the power either to enhance or to chip away at the prospects for your wealth, health, happiness, and overall well-being.

INTENTIONAL DESIGN

As you know, the nine areas of the Bagua are zones of energy, each representing a different aspect of your life, which can be strengthened or weakened at any moment by personal circumstances. The center gua, the position of power, represents the foundation for reaching your full potential. It comes naturally into balance when the other guas are balanced, and when harmony prevails there, it's like neutral gear in a car: you can move in any direction to focus on your life work with clarity and purpose.

If some part of your life is a little lacking in harmony, examine what part of the Bagua correlates to the situation. For example, if money were scarce, you'd first scrutinize the Wealth and Prosperity gua in your home or workplace to see if there was any correlation to what was going on. Let's say your Wealth corner is located in an unused or cluttered spare bedroom: the lack of stability there might correspond to the unsteady flow of money into your life.

What then? As a first step, you might make a change in the physical environment—changes such as those we discussed in Chapter 2. You would use the tools of feng shui—Yin and Yang, the Five Elements, and energy work. Perhaps you would choose to place a luxurious red chair in that room—or in the wealth corner of some other room—as a symbolic wealth enhancement with the intention of generating a prosperity-related result. If it worked, you might receive an unexpected check in the mail or be offered a new job. If nothing happened, you'd need to ask yourself whether that chair really meant "wealth" to you. If you don't buy into it—if it doesn't represent your perception of wealth or resonate with your desire—it's not going to bring results.

The *intention* you assign to every feng shui enhancement is the real power behind the practice. Intention works by visualizing what you sincerely want to accomplish and then applying a healthy dose of faith, hope, and passion to manifest the desired outcome. If you've done this—if your enhancements have meaning and are correctly placed within your space—and there's still no result, it's time to look inside yourself for the reasons why. And the same map that guides you around your physical space can show you the way within.

THE ROAD MAP OF YOUR LIFE

When I first became interested in the inner wisdom of feng shui—something that it seemed few people had given much thought to—I was looking for ways to explore what struck me as a deep and fascinating connection between inner work and outer work. It wasn't long before I discovered that the Bagua itself could chart the meeting points of the world without and the world within. This is why I like to say that the Bagua is both the treasure map of your home and the road map of your life.

To create my own version of the Bagua map—the Inner Wisdom Bagua (which you can download from www.ggRedecorating.com/articles)—was a five-year process of using intuition to probe beneath the surface of conventional practices and cures. I began by writing down key words and phrases associated with each gua. From there, I expanded the inquiry through reading, research, and intuitive work to help me determine what aspects of inner life resonated with each gua. On my teacher's advice, I worked with the *I Ching* every day, asking questions, finding the hexagrams to answer them—this can be done in several ways, such as with sticks or coins—and looking up the meaning of each, then writing out the questions and my interpretation of the answers in a journal.

For example, in examining the inner wisdom of the Love, Marriage, and Relationships gua, I asked about the concept of unconditional love, which is a common theme in books on love and relationships. My specific question focused on how to deal with a partner's emotional distance. The answer I received dispelled the concept of *unconditional*: it's just *love,* I was told, and relationships must have boundaries to retain balance. Unconditional love implies that you have to put up with bad behavior or be patient beyond what is normal, even if you're being treated poorly; real forgiveness means letting go of your attachment to an outcome or situation, not excusing someone for unconscious or poor behavior.

Ultimately, the Bagua I developed laid out the core concepts, personal practices, soul qualities, and vital lessons relevant to each space of our lives. I found, for example, that during my study of the *I Ching,* if I posed a question that had to do with the state of my finances, I would be redirected to core values of wealth and prosperity. These included perseverance, persistence, and optimism. The *I Ching* would also advise me to pursue a livelihood without greed, one that would help me but serve others at the same time. By living in sync with these qualities, I would guarantee that money would continue to flow.

The inner wisdom for each life area is laid out below:

WEALTH AND PROSPERITY "PERSISTENT WIND"
Core concepts: Perseverance, persistence, charity, livelihood without greed, service to others, appreciation, optimism
Personal practice: Count your blessings daily.
Soul qualities: Grateful attitude and focus on paying it forward
Vital lesson: If you always give, you'll always have.

FAME AND REPUTATION
"CLINGING FIRE"

Core concepts: Reputation, recognition, integrity, authenticity, legacy, sincerity, honesty, community, future

Personal practice: Identify your lasting legacy and choose every action in accordance with achieving that goal.

Soul qualities: Focus on achieving goals in harmony with your truth

Vital lesson: Walk your talk.

LOVE, MARRIAGE, AND RELATIONSHIPS
"RECEPTIVE EARTH"

Core concepts: Receptivity, self-love, compassion, romance, connection, passion, loving kindness, partnership

Personal practice: Cultivate your inner magnetism to draw in and keep relationships.

Soul qualities: An open mind, always coming from a place of love

Vital lesson: Love grows from the inside out.

HEALTH AND FAMILY
"SHOCKING THUNDER"

Core concepts: Strength, forgiveness, boundaries, discernment, flexibility, expression, intuition, cooperation, ancestors

Personal practice: Seek optimum physical, mental, emotional, and spiritual health.

Soul qualities: Emphasis on maintaining a strong family and friends of choice

Vital lesson: It's not what you're eating; it's what's eating you.

EARTH
"CENTER"

Core concepts: Balance, groundedness, unity, calm, connectedness, self-awareness, completion, harmony, enlightenment

Personal practice: Be conscious, present, and aware.

Soul qualities: Tuning in to your inner voice and harmonizing with your inner truth

Vital lesson: Love what is.

CREATIVITY AND CHILDREN
"JOYOUS LAKE"

Core concepts: Joy, creativity, focus, logic, encouragement, imagination, originality

Personal practice: Laugh, dance, create, paint, sing, play.

Soul qualities: Joy from within, passion that creates discipline, willingness to nurture your inner child

Vital lesson: Dream with your eyes open.

KNOWLEDGE AND SELF-CULTIVATION
"STILL MOUNTAIN"

Core concepts: Quietude, reflection, peace, contemplation, wisdom, meditation, stillness, introspection

Personal practice: Have some daily quiet time.

Soul qualities: Ability to redirect your energy to quieting the monkey mind

Vital lesson: Introspection leads to wisdom.

CAREER AND LIFE PURPOSE
"DEEP WATER"

Core concepts: Courage, trust, depth, life purpose, life work

Personal practice: Listen to your inner voice and honor your soul's desire.

Soul qualities: Finding the path of least resistance, pursuing your passion, and surrendering to your inner guidance system

Vital lesson: Chase the inspiration, not the money.

HELPFUL PEOPLE AND TRAVEL
"CREATIVE HEAVEN"

Core concepts: Clarity, confidence, synchronicity, spirituality, patience, insight, maturity

Personal practice: Seek resonant spiritual guidance, helpers, teachers, mentors.

Soul qualities: Openness to the guidance of synchronicity

Vital lesson: You are always where you need to be.

We humans constantly search for new ways to find peace, whether that means a trip to a remote beach or a secluded mountain retreat, a yoga class, or just a long walk. Yet all too often, the moment we're back in the whirlwind of activity that occupies our lives, that peaceful feeling begins to evaporate. I believe that the ability (or inability) to maintain that sense of peace can be attributed to the condition of the nine guas, since they magnify the condition of every aspect of our lives, shining a spotlight to show us where we are in life. As a result, the Inner Wisdom Bagua can help us assess and redirect the energy of each gua with focus and optimism. I don't suggest attacking the energy directly with, say, mantras or affirmations designed to change behavior or point of view; these won't work if we have any doubts about the statements. Instead, I prefer a process of self-examination. Think back to the example of Wealth and Prosperity (the nonworking red chair). Examining your feelings about money may highlight a particular thought or belief you're holding on to that hinders your ability to attract it. Or maybe you define wealth narrowly as the accumulation of material goods, limiting your ability to appreciate other riches readily available to you, such as good health or abundant friendships.

Working with the Inner Wisdom Bagua is a process of examining attitudes and core beliefs, then making enhancements in your inner world that are reflected and supported by the world you form around you. With this powerful process, you can convert any space into a sacred place to cultivate your ambition; determine your purpose; and find stability, clarity, and peace.

In the chapters ahead, we'll focus on each area of the Bagua map to access the inner wisdom that's available to you in every aspect of your life. We will focus on enhancing the soul qualities associated with each gua to help you grow in all these areas. At the same time, I'll help you support your inner process by enhancing your environment in ways that make sense for you. Remember sometimes the work that needs to be done to solve a problem deals more with the internal than the external. This means that the work isn't necessarily done in the specific physical gua associated with your problem; sometimes it must take place in a seemingly unrelated area of your home, and sometimes we'll look at enhancing one section of each gua, room by room.

Using the Bagua map tool, I will show you how to fine-tune each part of your life, restoring, balancing, or stimulating the energy associated with it. By identifying the aspects of your life that give you the least satisfaction, you'll be able to ascertain how these are represented and anchored in the internal and external environment, both positively and negatively. Let's look at love, marriage, and relationships as an example. If I were doing a consultation for someone who felt lacking in love, the process would go like this:

- I would scrutinize the condition of the Love, Marriage, and Relationships gua on the property, in the house, and within each room.

- I would look at the overall energy of love throughout the space to detect whether this quality is fully represented or clearly deficient.

- I would look at specific rooms that embody the energy of this quality. For example, I would focus on the bedroom—no matter which gua it resides in.

- And finally, I would look at the mind-sets of the individuals residing in the space to see how they are contributing to the outcome.

Once you have evaluated these four things and pinpointed any problems, you can begin rebuilding the energy of each life aspect using both internal and external feng shui.

As we examine each gua, I'll explain its core concepts and philosophy and share some examples of how my clients have enhanced it to improve their lives. Then I'll offer a set of soul-searching questions designed to help you start your self-examination and get to your own truth, one that's as unique as a fingerprint. The consciousness shifts to alert status the moment you start questioning in this particular way, and these questions will trigger your own intuition—your inner truth—to kick in; they'll help you become aware of the patterns in your life, determine whether you're satisfied with the results, and recognize what changes need to take place. You can also create your own questions to correspond with specific issues in your life.

I recommend that you approach this as you might approach a project: read about all nine guas before answering any of the questions. Once you've done that and are ready to start, work on one gua at a time. You may want to start with the gua that needs the most attention. For example, if cash flow is a challenge, you might focus on the Wealth and Prosperity gua first to dismantle old failures and draft a new model. Alternatively, you can follow the order I often suggest to clients:

- Master bedroom
- Entryways (front door, foyer, and the room you enter from the garage)
- Center of the home (Earth)
- Wealth and Prosperity
- Love, Marriage, and Relationships

You'll want to work on all nine guas eventually, but you have to start somewhere! Setting priorities lets you proceed methodically through the Bagua map, finding a sense of completion from each gua in turn until you are finished—and experiencing along the way the blessings and magical moments that feng shui brings.

PART III

Wealth & Prosperity

"Persistent Wind"

Core concepts: Perseverance, persistence, charity, livelihood without greed, service to others, appreciation, optimism

Personal practice: Count your blessings daily.

Soul qualities: Grateful attitude, and focus on paying it forward

Vital lesson: If you always give, you'll always have.

Colors: Blues, purples, reds

Enhancements: Books and quotes on gratitude, expensive or precious jewelry, piggy banks, amethyst crystals, and artwork symbolic of prosperity.

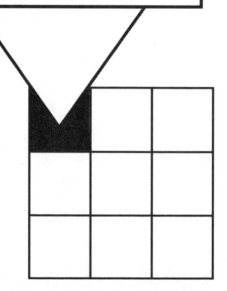

CHAPTER 6

ACCESSING ABUNDANCE

The Wealth and Prosperity Gua

In the confrontation between the stream and the rock, the stream always wins—not through strength but by perseverance.

— H. JACKSON BROWN

My client Shirley, a successful entrepreneur, had an upbeat and optimistic personality. Her live-in boyfriend, by contrast, viewed everything in life as the glass half empty. His focus always seemed to be on what was not working for him, whether it was the growth of his business, his money flow, or the condition of his personal relationships. When he and Shirley had lived together for about a year, she began to notice that her business was weakening—and her personal life, in which she had balanced work and free time, getting together often with girlfriends and making time for meditation and journaling, began to suffer too. She became increasingly aware of her own focus on cash flow, a gradual decline in new clients and business opportunities, and a deterioration in her generally optimistic point of view about the ebb and flow of life.

Feeling a bit out of sorts, Shirley called me for a feng shui consultation to help her identify the link between her living situation and the downward spiral that her livelihood was taking. Since both she and her boyfriend worked from home, my first move was to find out where their offices were located within the Bagua map of their home and then evaluate the design of each office. This was the focus of my work because the office is the room that most embodies the energy of Wealth and Prosperity, no matter which gua it is in. In addition to focusing on the office, I needed to look at the Wealth and Prosperity gua to be sure that there were no obvious blocks to the energy there.

When I evaluated their home, I found that they shared an office, located in the Health and Family gua. In general, I don't recommend sharing an office with another if you can avoid it, unless you both have the same vocation and it requires you to work in sync with each other. It is too likely that the energy can become divided, which was precisely Shirley's situation. Though the room was well-lit, windowed, and spacious enough for two, the differing natures of their jobs—his involved maintaining many relationships, talking on the phone, and so on, while hers was insular and required great focus—made the setup bad for both of them. Shirley's attention was being pulled away from her work, and her boyfriend didn't feel comfortable operating as he would like to because he didn't want to be distracting.

Now that I knew the situation, I asked Shirley how much time she actually spent in her office. It was no surprise that she answered, "Very little." As we talked, she realized she was spending more and more time away from her home office in order to remove herself from the distractions. She had "unplugged" from her business as a coping mechanism, rather than putting her energy into growing it, and it was affecting her career.

The treatment was to separate the offices so that both of them could regain control over their respective sources of revenue and the running of their businesses. Happily, Shirley's boyfriend chose this time to move his office out of their home into a new location. For Shirley, it was as if a dark cloud had disappeared, leaving stillness and clarity in its place.

With half the room empty now that his desk and file cabinets were gone, we had a great opportunity to rethink the space along good feng shui lines. I first recommended a thorough cleaning and decluttering of the office, removing any accessories or furniture that could be managed easily—anything that didn't require a moving van and a team of handlers! This would have been a great time to apply a fresh coat of paint, if one were needed; since it wasn't, Shirley just cleaned the room top to bottom with nontoxic, ecofriendly products. Then we set out to fill the space consciously, right down to the shelves and drawers, replacing old file folders with new ones in the colors of wealth and prosperity—red, purple, and blue.

Shirley needed additional storage, and an Asian-inspired cabinet in black lacquer and gold fit perfectly where her boyfriend's desk had been. On top of the cabinet I added classical feng shui enhancements for upward growth, protection, and security, such as a green glass turtle and a bamboo plant in a red heart vase. On the wall above it, I placed several colorful watercolors that Shirley had painted, as a way to further spark her creative and artistic ambitions.

After enhancing the energy of her office, I looked at the actual Wealth and Prosperity gua of Shirley's home, which was located in the master bathroom. This created an additional dynamic of prosperity "going down the drain." To prevent this, I recommended that Shirley maintain a daily habit of keeping the toilet lid down, the sink and bathtub drains closed, and the shower drain covered. I also helped her improve the energy with new coat of paint in deep gold hue and embellishments that represented wealth to Shirley, including red towels, a jewelry box, and healthy plants.

By putting a special focus on the wealth and prosperity in her office and getting rid of energy drains in her Wealth and Prosperity gua, it wasn't long before her stagnant business quickly turned itself around to an abundant flow. Like energy attracts like energy, and once she redirected her energy toward abundance, new business opportunities naturally followed. She was amazed at how quickly she saw results!

THE INNER WISDOM OF WEALTH

Traditionally, wealth and prosperity in feng shui means just that—the flow of money. While that's certainly an important aspect of this gua (and, undeniably, of our modern lives), I like to expand the definition of abundance beyond the mere accumulation of assets. There's wealth to be found in all areas of your life: good health, loyal family and friends, your children and pets, nature's bounty and beauty. You can live in a tent and consider yourself wealthy if you take this view.

When I was developing my Inner Wisdom Bagua, working with the *I Ching* to discern the qualities of each gua at the level of inner wisdom, what I learned about wealth and prosperity ultimately had more to do with giving than with getting. The cycle of prosperity gains momentum in direct proportion to your generosity toward others. When you give freely, without conditions, prosperity is paid forward, and this creates an opportunity for it to return to you at a later time, often when you need it the most. Keep the wheel turning with acts of charity and straightforward acts of kindness. If you want to attract more money, try donating some of *your* money, time, or talent to an organization that works for those who are less fortunate. If you see someone struggling with a heavy box, help him or her carry the load. The great lesson of this gua—and the spirit in which we can actively enhance it—is simple: if you always give, you'll always have.

There's another side to this coin (no pun intended). As long as you perceive money as a limited resource in short supply, you'll endlessly strive to get your share; as long as you define wealth solely in terms of amassing money, you'll have to work around the clock in order to enjoy life. And though we all need a certain amount of money to sustain even a simple lifestyle, sooner or later you'll have to confront the question, *how much is enough?*

We are making choices about wealth every day, sometimes without even knowing we have a choice. If we think the economy is in the toilet, we may hoard our money. If we think we deserve to have expensive gadgets or home upgrades because we work hard or because somehow they'll make life better, or because we want to raise our status with neighbors and friends, then we may spend beyond our means, which usually means spending on credit. In fact, either way—whether you have a lack of faith in your financial future or continue to operate in denial by spending more than you can afford—what you're effectively doing is hoarding, and hoarding shuts down the flow of energy and ultimately of opportunities.

Hoarding is a lack of faith, a lack of trust that the Universe will provide for you exactly when you need it, which is the crucial piece of inner wisdom this gua offers. Just because we have to make do with less, that doesn't translate into disaster. It simply challenges us to find new ways of doing things and to have faith that the pendulum will swing the other way. We should be focused on the lesson that is being revealed during a financial crunch, not on the crunch itself.

National credit-card debt is likely to surpass the $1 trillion mark, with a fair number of those card users defaulting rather than paying up. And this debt doesn't just create mental clutter—the worry of bills and finance charges, the energy it takes to keep the worry at bay—it often creates literal clutter too. The next time you're about to buy something and charge it to a credit card, whether it's an object you'll have to find a place for or a gadget you'll feel guilty if you don't use, ask yourself, *Is this purchase going to add clutter to my life in any way?* Remember, clutter has a purpose! It's either keeping you tethered to the past or creating a daydream about the future. The more you accumulate, the more you become a slave to the need to keep it all in order. Any way you look at it, it's ultimately robbing you of your freedom. We may think that accumulating, be it material goods or money in the bank, will help us feel safe and secure; we may think we need it to support our self-esteem or even to tell us who we are. True security, though, comes from *knowing* who we are, what we are capable of, and what we are meant to do during our time on this earth. And a true awareness of abundance comes from focusing on what you do have instead of what you don't: gratitude can be as much a wealth magnet as giving.

Gratitude means being aware of all the things for which you can give thanks in the course of a day— your health, a sunny morning, a compliment you receive, a smooth ride to work. It helps to raise your awareness of these blessings if you write them down daily in a journal or recite them to yourself before you go to bed. Complaining about everything that *isn't* going well for you is the same as being ungrateful for what *is* going right; focusing solely on the negative reinforces the notion that some part of your life isn't good enough. If you find yourself immersed in worry and negative thoughts throughout the day, ask yourself if it's helping to make things any better.

Working with Wealth and Prosperity

The nine guas of the Bagua, as you know, are zones of energy that can be strengthened or weakened at any moment by personal circumstances. Each of the guas represents a different aspect of life that requires attention, and each has unique characteristics represented by symbols, shapes, colors, materials, and elements. By manipulating objects in your physical space, you're bringing the energy into balance with the natural flow of life. This energy is at work in your life, no matter where you find yourself!

On the Bagua map, Wealth and Prosperity is found in the rear left corner, with the "front" being the wall that contains the entrance. This map can be overlaid on your home in several ways—on the whole property (if you're in a house on a lot), the whole building (if you're in an apartment), the house or apartment itself, each room within it, and each surface within each room—and you can enhance the energy of Wealth and Prosperity at any level. You find the wealth corner by applying the Bagua map to a room or a surface such as a desktop, just as you apply it to your whole floor plan, aligning the bottom of the Bagua with the front edge of the surface or the wall that contains the door to the room. You're also enhancing the Wealth gua whenever you do anything that supports its qualities in your inner life: counting your blessings, being of service, paying it forward with whatever you can afford to give.

Enhancing a gua in your physical environment involves balancing its energy using the tools we laid out in Chapter 2: the Five Elements and the essential equation of Yin and Yang. The front third of a home, at the bottom of the Bagua map, is associated with vigorous Yang energy, since this is the area exposed to the active outside world, the place where traffic comes through the front door. The rear third, away from traffic, is the quieter domain of Yin energy, passive and restful. The Wealth gua, in the rear, is by nature a Yin area, so Yin energy is the one to improve when you want to invite prosperity in. Yin is supported by elements of décor including warm colors, wood furniture, soft fabrics, and muted lighting, and by activities that restore energy, such as sleep and self-care. Decorative elements such as plants, ceiling fans, and electronics shift the balance toward Yang, as do active functions such as reading, watching television, and exercising.

Proper feng shui balance involves working with the Five Elements as well. Wealth and Prosperity is associated with the Fire element; if you find that your cash flow is ebbing or it's hard to come by the money you need for sustenance, then it's time to bring more Fire into the space, say, in the form of candles or the color red—as well as to "fire up" the key wisdom points of the gua. These are elements of appreciation and gratitude for all the blessings in your life, including anything that is going well for you, such as family and friends who support you; observation and acknowledgment (as opposed to envy or resentment) of others who are doing well, whether you know them or not; giving of yourself in the form of money, time, or talent; and decluttering your mind of any notions of lack and replacing them with a consciousness of service.

As powerful as the classic feng shui considerations are, it's equally important to consider the visual and emotional energy of your environment—the messages that your home gives you every minute and sends out through you into the world. Any object in your environment that might come across as deteriorating or unhealthy is sending a message that undermines prosperity: dead leaves, dead plants, empty plant pots; any object that needs repair; any piece of clothing that doesn't fit you or needs repair or cleaning before you can wear it; a piggy bank that has no money in it or that you haven't been adding to consistently. Photos of people who do not support you or who are no longer in your life (but are still living) work against prosperity, as does clutter of any kind. Stacking your bills to be paid all at once, instead of paying them one at a time as they come in, works against wealth, as does failure to notice all the blessings present in every day—such as a good night's sleep, a sunny morning, a compliment, a self-less gesture from someone else.

Feng shui works on all these levels, as well as on every level of your physical environment, from small to large, and a total program of transformation needs to take in all of it. I'll use my own home as an example. If I wanted to focus on dramatically improving prosperity, I would need to enhance the Wealth and Prosperity gua of the property, the whole home, and each room in the home, as well as the qualities and questions that give access to the inner wisdom of wealth: in other words, a complete and concentrated program for attracting abundance.

The wealth corner on my property is mostly out of my control, since I live in a community where the homeowners' association manages the grounds, including the property around each house. (Someone living in an apartment or a condo would have a similar situation.) I don't have a yard per se, and I can't just plant a tree or place a statue. What I can control is a bit of landscaping near the house. So I've buried two pointed energy crystals at the very edge of the wealth area—crystals are powerful energy boosters, and the points send energy upward, where I want my prosperity to go—and I make sure the plant growth prospers by keeping it well tended and healthy.

The wealth corner of my house is the master bathroom, which is usually a feng shui don't: wealth is challenged daily by being "flushed" down the toilet or drain. So I've spent a lot of time on the décor of this room, using both contemporary feng shui enhancements (gold metallic color on the walls, red towels, healthy plants such as jade and bamboo, motivational sayings in frames on the walls) and traditional gestures (red envelopes in the room's wealth corner, a turtle with a dragon head sitting on money). The reasons behind these enhancements are no great mystery: gold and red are wealth colors, gold to represent the literal aspect of gold and red to fire up or ignite prosperity; the emerald-colored jade plant has fat leaves that actually store water, and water is the element that represents career, which is intimately connected to wealth; the bamboo plant grows easily and is quite content with little, and both plants are classical feng shui remedies in China. Red envelopes—another representation of fire energy—can have either money or a saying placed inside them; they represent an ancient good-luck custom and show that nothing is left to chance. The turtle embodies security and protection, and it's a powerful emblem of feng shui in itself, as it is believed that the design on the back of the turtle's shell represents the nine areas of the Bagua map. The dragon head in place of a turtle head is adding fire energy that turns dreams into reality. No animal is more closely associated with feng shui than the dragon—it is like a guardian angel—and by sitting on money, it is protecting the wealth I accumulate over time. Though I don't recommend using traditional feng shui cures across the board, these work for me because, through my work and study, I've invested them with intention and meaning. As a result, the room feels luxurious, like a spa—a place where I care for myself and so does my partner.

In the Wealth and Prosperity gua of each room of my house, no matter what gua the room is in, I keep objects, artwork, or accessories that reflect wealth. My favorite is a ceramic vase made by a local artist, in which I store lucky pennies I find on the street; for me, it represents the slow accumulation of wealth over time. On surfaces such as my dresser, desktop, and meditation table, I've placed similar symbolic wealth gestures. And in my quiet time, when I'm meditating or just thinking, I try to reflect on the inner qualities of wealth—gratitude, charity, service, perseverance, patience—to see if I'm keeping the gua active with positive thought, intention, and action. That's the full program—I leave nothing to chance!

FINDING THE GIFTS

Some years ago, I became aware of a dawning worry: that I would run out of time for all the things I wanted to experience in my life if I didn't make an effort now. My wish list included exotic travel, unforgettable adventures, and meeting extraordinary people. I was working at ESPN at the time, and my high-powered corporate career left little to no time for a personal life, so even having time to dream was a luxury. Even though on some level I sensed that I'd probably live to be 103, I proceeded to make a list of "50 Things to Do Before I Die"—the kind of thing that's often referred to as a Bucket List. Taking the time to write down each wish made me realize that there had to be a corresponding piece of my life that felt unfulfilled, and that I didn't dare postpone happiness any longer.

The first item on my list was learning how to snowboard. I flew out to the beautiful Colorado mountains and immersed myself in snowboarding lessons. Already an accomplished snow skier, I figured snowboarding would be a snap, and it was. After the first few days of lessons, I was having the time of my life and even contemplated trying out for ESPN's Winter Extreme Games. Did they even have a category over 40?

Then, on the fourth day of my extreme snowboarding career, I fell, breaking two bones in my left arm and tearing most of the ligaments in my left hand. I was laid up for several months while enduring multiple casts and follow-up surgeries, and I had ample time to contemplate the gift I had been given as a result of this accident.

First, I had to ask for help to do just about anything, something I was not inherently good at. Friends drove me to work, assisted me in getting dressed and styling my hair, and helped me with day-to-day chores and errands. It was amazing to see how my loving friends and co-workers jumped at every opportunity to pitch in. I became aware that if I didn't accept and receive help when I needed it most, I robbed others of their joy in being of service to a friend in need. Gratitude is the essence of wealth and prosperity, and gratitude for the gift of reliable friends enriches the givers too.

As I was approaching my birthday this year, I decided to forgo parties, balloons, and confetti. Instead, I was determined to move on to another item on my Bucket List—paddleboarding. It seemed like a perfect way to spend my Sunday birthday, communing with nature; a bit like surfing without the drama and sharks! I arranged for the rental of a paddleboard and a private lesson. The night before, I was so excited I couldn't sleep, and I arrived at the launch site an hour early to soak in the early morning sunshine and take pleasure in the peaceful waves along the bay.

An hour passed, then two, but my paddleboard instructor never showed. *Wow,* I thought, *a no-show on my birthday? Now what is the nature of* this *gift?* I knew there must be one. I drove home, had a lovely nap, and enjoyed a beautiful day. I was excited, of course, to see what that birthday gift would reveal, all in good time.

The next day, I took my car to the auto shop for some routine repairs. The owner offered to drive me to a restaurant so that I could pass the time until the car repair was finished. On the way, he asked me what was new, so I proceeded to tell him about being stood up for a paddleboard lesson that I had paid for in advance, and on my birthday, no less! He seemed horrified, but I told him not to fret, as I'd still had a magical day.

When I returned to pick up my car and asked what the total would be, the owner exclaimed, "Happy Birthday!" I thanked him and asked again how much the repair cost. "Your money is no good here!" Then I got it—this was the lovely, unexpected gift. His self-less gesture of generosity meant more to me than a commercial paddleboard lesson! And one of my girl-friends, who is a paddleboard enthusiast, offered to teach me instead. Knowing that there is a gift in every situation is a crucial component of a wealthy life: it leaves no room for lack, disappointment, or despair.

SELF-INQUIRY: WEALTH FROM THE INSIDE OUT

I try to cultivate a consciousness of abundance all the time now, not only when things are going well, but also—especially—when they aren't. If I feel that money is tight or business is slow, I may ask myself, *Have I been paying it forward with my time, talent, or money? Have I been actively pursuing ways of generating new business, or am I just sitting around pouting?* And I try to stay alert for the gift in every situation that comes my way.

You can scrutinize your personal connection to wealth and prosperity in much the same way in your own life. Use the questions below—or questions you come up with, specific to your own concerns—to help you become aware of your patterns, see if you're satisfied with the results, and recognize the changes that need to take place. The questions below are the triggers for your intuition to operate and your inner truth to reveal itself.

- Do I have enough money to do what I need to do today?

- Is it easy or difficult for me to earn money?

- Do I feel I have sufficient resources to provide for myself and my family?

- Does money seem to slip through my fingers?

- Do I often feel anxious about money or envious of others who have more of it than I do?

- How do I define success?

- How do I feel when I receive an unexpected bill? What about an unexpected check?

- Am I meeting my goals and aspirations—financial or otherwise?

- Do I share my blessings with others who are less fortunate?

- Am I taking the necessary steps to secure my future?

- Am I spending beyond my means?

- Do I feel I need wealth to gain social status or approval?

- Am I making a difference in other people's lives?

Every question you formulate should be simple, precise, and relevant to your life. Any question that looks outward and not inward is not going to serve you well. *What's going to happen in the stock market this year? Will I ever get that raise? Why have I had to work harder than my friends (neighbors, siblings, co-workers) to get where I am?* These questions are based either in the future or in the past, and they're about external circumstances, not your inner life. If you are working on examining your own values and developing deep gratitude for the wealth you enjoy in all its forms, you'll be able to keep the wheel of prosperity turning, bringing abundance into your life in the same way you offer it to the world.

Fame & Reputation

"Clinging Fire"

Core concepts: Reputation, recognition, integrity, authenticity, legacy, sincerity, honesty, community, future

Personal practice: Identify your lasting legacy and choose every action in accordance with achieving that goal.

Soul qualities: Focus on achieving goals in harmony with your truth

Vital lesson: Walk your talk.

Colors: Reds

Enhancements: Books, quotes, and artwork related to your integrity, reputation, and creative works. Lighting and candles.

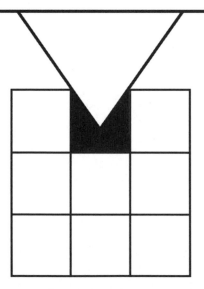

CHAPTER 7

SHAPING YOUR LEGACY

The Fame and Reputation Gua

Life is like a game of cards. The hand that is dealt to you represents determinism, the way you play it is free will.

— JAWAHARLAL NEHRU

The nine guas of the Bagua map—just like the areas of your life—are intimately intertwined. This means that sometimes the imbalance that is keeping you from experiencing the success you want may lie in an area of your life that seems to have a less direct connection to the problem you're facing. This is exactly what happened to my client Jeff in his quest for love and marriage. We found that his imbalance lay more in his Fame and Reputation gua than in Love, Marriage, and Relationships.

Jeff was a single 38-year-old, newly promoted to vice president of his electronics company. His friends maintained that he was married to his job, although he dated when time permitted—mostly when he needed a date for corporate functions. He was building his personal empire of success, concentrating on particular goals: a bigger house, a faster car, and a vacation condo as an investment. In his words, this was the landscape necessary to attract the right gal to settle down with and have a family. He was very clear about the image he was projecting into the world, and it was proving very effective—but what was the effect?

Jeff received a gift certificate for my services as a Christmas present from one of my clients, his mother. At first he was skeptical, and I could tell he was quite surprised when I arrived at his door in corporate business attire! We began by talking about what his goals were in life, and I discovered that they centered around getting married and out of the singles-bar scene. Then he took me on a tour.

As I assessed his floor plan room by room, I noted that the overall energy and décor of Jeff's home were focused on solo accomplishments, comfort, and personal appeal. I asked him if he'd had the assistance of an interior designer when he put his home together, and he said he had.

"Did you give her a theme or vision for the choices in your décor?" I asked.

"Yes," he said. "I told her I wanted a fabulous bachelor pad." The interior designer had sure done her job—and this is what had brought about his reputation as a swinging single. It was also the source of his imbalance. His goals and his environment didn't match. If he had wanted to remain single and focus only on work, there would have been no problem. However, that wasn't the case.

When I pointed out the examples of furniture, artwork, and accessories in each room that were anchoring his bachelorhood, Jeff had to laugh. The "bachelor" signals ranged from one leather recliner facing an oversized TV that was the focal point of the living quarters (where was Ms. Right going to sit?) to artwork of exotic women in sultry poses throughout the home. While he could see the specific correlations between these items and what was currently going on in his life, he didn't immediately buy into how changing the point of view in his home would energetically influence the way he moved through the world.

"Try looking at it this way," I said. "As a leader in new business development, aren't you encouraged to take risks or leaps of faith?" I suggested that he try out a rearrangement of his existing furniture and buy some new things that better represented his future goals. He was to live with the changes I recommended for two months and then, if he didn't like them or wasn't comfortable, he could change everything back. With permission to change things back to the way they were after a period of time, he decided to commit to the plan.

So we took a three-pronged attack: tone down the bachelor energy of his overall design, enhance his Love, Marriage, and Relationships gua, and focus on his Fame and Reputation gua by incorporating symbols representing the life he wanted.

In the living room, I softened the black leather and the steely look of the furniture with colorful silk pillows and end-table accessories in warm tones of red and gold. I swapped out the black-and-white geometric throw rug for a multicolored contemporary rug to anchor the furniture. The furniture itself got rearranged in a U-shape to foster conversation instead of being angled toward the big-screen TV on the wall. (There is a feng shui joke that the bigger the TV, the faster the divorce. Even feng shui has a humorous side!)

In the master bedroom—a very important room to focus on for love and marriage, even if it isn't in the Love, Marriage, and Relationships gua—we transformed the repetitive pattern of black, white, and steel with a new wood bed frame and contemporary but functional dark wood end tables topped with ceramic lamp bases in a deep red hue with textured lampshades. A new chenille bedspread added subtle romantic flair in a swirl of complementary colors—red, gold, and taupe—to complete the transformation. The pictures of single exotic females were replaced with a variety of modern and traditional prints, each showing two or more figures or objects, the better to represent "pairs."

While in many cases it's important to focus on the gua of the life aspect you're trying to improve, sometimes, this is the least of your concerns. This was the case for Jeff, because the Love, Marriage, and Relationships gua of his home was a rarely used guest room. I did accessorize this in the same manner as his master bedroom; however, because it wasn't used very often, it was more important to apply the energy enhancements throughout the home—in well-used areas—to keep the energy active. By displaying the feeling of Love, Marriage, and Relationships throughout, the energy of love is continually activated.

Once the new décor was in place, Jeff began to see the difference in the energy of his home. Having moved away from his bachelor pad to an intimate and inviting setting, he observed a key correlation: focusing on the acquisition of material goods in his home would be more likely to attract materialistic women into his life. In fact, he was clear that a relationship with a woman focused on material things was *not* what he wanted. He wanted a romantic partner to share his adventures.

With his image as a romantic partner taking better shape, it was time to look at another piece of the puzzle—the larger legacy he was creating with his life and how much satisfaction it was (or wasn't) bringing him. This was the reputation he needed to develop. While Jeff loved his job, his direction was focused on static goals: house, car, gadgets. Static goals (which are essentially passive energy) provide one-time moments of temporary happiness. Once you have them, you're on to looking for something bigger, something better. Choosing "motion goals" (active energy) that are purpose-driven, such as ambitions that serve others, are perpetually rewarding. They shift the focus from self to selfless. To address this aspect of his Fame and Reputation, I suggested that Jeff add some volunteer activities on weekends with like-minded people and let the experience unfold to see where it would take him.

Jeff joined an organization devoted to promoting green living, personal growth, and fitness, all things he was interested in himself. As a volunteer, he used his business acumen and organization skills to start up a natural living fair in his community. In the process of organizing the event, he met a lovely woman, and they are now in a committed, monogamous relationship. He has let me know that he is spending a lot less time in front of the TV and enjoying the companionship of his girlfriend. He keeps me up to date with his joyful life and calls me the "feng shui lady" who helped transform it.

WORKING WITH FAME AND REPUTATION

The Fame and Reputation gua of your home, located in the middle rear of the Bagua map, is an energy center shining your light out into the world. This is the place to display objects or accessories that represent achievement, either on your own part or by those you admire. It's also an ideal place to hang diplomas and other honors—unless your Fame and Reputation area happens to include your master bedroom. Your bedroom is not meant to be a shrine to you alone; it's about you in relationship to others, and it should reflect the energy of a couple (even if you don't share it with a partner). You'll read more about this in the next chapter. Fame and Reputation, on the other hand, *is* all about you as a unique individual: your qualifications, your credentials, your accomplishments, and the mentors and inspiring figures who help you to achieve.

Fame and Reputation sits right next to Wealth and Prosperity, and there's a reciprocal relationship between them: living a life of generous giving is bound to build your reputation, and as your reputation rises, business opportunities may increase, thanks to the support of all those who know your value. Like Wealth and Prosperity, the Fame and Reputation gua is associated with the Fire element, which you can power up with candles, crystals, and pyramids (symbolic of a campfire shape) made from precious minerals. These enhancements, along with lighting, energize any area they're placed in, and they also boost the energy of other objects around them. So if you want to give your reputation a boost, for example, you might place an amethyst crystal next to a photo of you with a successful friend or entrepreneur, someone who's famous in your field, or anyone you welcome being associated with. Equally important is to avoid symbolic objects that create negative visual energy to pull your reputation down, however inadvertently. Posters of cartoon or cinema villains send the wrong message (that's not how you want to be seen!); skulls suggest a reputation that's dead or dying; and images of people without all their body parts in place (not as grisly as it sounds—think of a Picasso painting or a Greek sculpture sans arms) could indicate that something's missing or truncated in the image you present to the world.

Fame, too, is by nature a Yin quality and calls for an area suited for quiet activities, enhanced by warm colors, wood furniture, gentle light, and soft finishes. It's an ideal place for an office, as well as a good place for a guest room, a living room, or a porch or lanai where you relax and restore yourself. It's not ideal for a bathroom—your reputation could go "down the drain"—but you may not have any control over where the plumbing is located in your home, so this inauspicious use of the gua can be balanced out with especially deliberate decorating. The same is true for bedrooms: they can work in this gua if they're properly enhanced. As I mentioned above, it's best not to place a master bedroom in Fame and Reputation; in my own home, though, that's exactly where the master bedroom is. So I save my diplomas and certificates for the walls of my office, acknowledging this gua in that space instead. In the bedroom, I embellish my image as an interior decorator and designer of ideal spaces by creating a beautiful, spa-like room that's peaceful, restful, and romantic. Further romantic gestures in the décor—photos of couples, objects in pairs—enhance my reputation as a romantic partner too.

BEING YOUR BEST

Fame and Reputation deals with the strength of your character and the way you appear to others. A reputation is built over time, teeter-tottering on the opinions and conclusions of acquaintances, co-workers, friends, neighbors, and family. Like it or not, our words and actions automatically come under scrutiny (and often criticism) every minute of the day. Some people remember every declaration and deed, be it good or bad. Others are more forgiving when behavior is less than stellar.

If you want to know the status of *your* fame and reputation, try asking friends or family how they would describe you to someone they know who has never met you. Encourage them to be frank. Then jot down some notes on how you want to be known based on the feedback you receive. Try doing this as if you were writing a speech recognizing you as the exemplary person of the year. Compare your notes with your friends' notes and see where there are gaps you need to bridge. Use the same technique with colleagues and peers at your workplace to gather information about how they see you as an employee, manager, or team player. Remember that the foundation of a first-class reputation is integrity, which includes being trustworthy, honest, and reliable. You gain power and respect in the world by being true to your word. You build your reputation over time, even moment by moment, based on your authenticity and willingness to expand. To put it another way, a good reputation reflects your authentic self, not your efforts to match society's definition of a successful person. Your ability to grow—*expand* is the word I like—depends on being open to constructive criticism, honest self-assessment, and the possibility of evolving to higher levels of compassion and modesty.

Dealing with my mother's Alzheimer's disease was an opportunity for me to expand beyond old expectations and beliefs (*Others should take care of people, not me; I don't have the energy or desire, and I wouldn't be good at it anyway*) and examine how I wanted to be known as a caretaker. When my mom was first diagnosed, in the early stages of the disease, she had trouble with short-term memory. Just a few minutes after eating breakfast, she would ask, "Have I had breakfast yet?" Frustrated, my dad and I would try to help her re-create the memory by providing details of the meal. My mom's puzzled expression made me realize how frustrating it was for her, too, to lose her recollection of something so routine.

I came to consider it an honor to care for my mother. I wanted to treat her with compassion and understanding, not frustration and denial. Eventually I noticed that she felt most herself when she wasn't struggling to remember five minutes ago, but just living and interacting in the moment. This was now her best, her new normal. I started to ask myself what *my* best in this new situation might be. If I could be my best in the present moment, I could better deal with whatever lay ahead. In order to do this, I discovered that I needed a restful night of sleep, some quiet time to myself, and enhancements in my surroundings to restore my energy and sense of balance. All this helped me to meet my mother in the moment, building a new "reputation" for myself from the inside out. Now if she asks me whether she's eaten breakfast, I respond with, "Are you hungry?" and we go from there.

Your Lasting Legacy

An integral part of Fame and Reputation is keeping an eye on your future by actively creating your legacy. You build a lasting legacy by making the contributions that are right for you, wherever you are in your life at that time. One way to enhance your reputation is to contribute to the well-being of family members, friends, or charitable organizations through a will, trust, savings program, or life insurance plan. But you don't have to rely on becoming wealthy to be remembered for making a contribution, and you don't have to be famous per se. Simply raising well-adjusted and compassionate children is a worthwhile and lasting legacy. In truth, every moment holds the possibility of leaving the world a better place than you found it; in every interaction you have with everyone you meet, you can make someone's day brighter.

Ultimately, all the areas of your life—all the corners of the Inner Wisdom Bagua map—play a role in building your life's legacy, because tending to them all with intention and care brings your whole life into balance so that your light can shine. The thing to remember is that *you* have immediate control over the way you'll be remembered and honored in the future—you're not leaving it up to luck or fate.

The word *fate* is often used interchangeably with *destiny* to mean a sequence of events that is predictable, inevitable, and unchangeable; you have no choice in the course of events because the outcome has been predetermined, with no room left for the action of free will. In the feng shui conception of destiny, by contrast, all that happens in your life is a result of your own actions. Your life is created by the choices you make, and your role is to bring blessings and tragedies into balance. Your imagination allows you to dream of better things, guiding your desire to reach your full potential and be all you are destined to be. At one time, it was a widely accepted belief that every situation and encounter *was* governed by destiny; however, this narrow point of view gives little or no consideration to the uniqueness of who you are today, right here, right now, and how you can create an amazing legacy through the choices you freely make.

SELF-INQUIRY: FAME FROM THE INSIDE OUT

Being aware of how you're conducting yourself in the present moment puts you in the best position to predict—and control—how you will conduct yourself in the next moment, and moment by moment is how a reputation is built and the foundation for a lasting legacy is laid. The goal is to operate from a calm, collected, composed, and unbiased position so you can respond intelligently and thoughtfully as needed or required. Use the questions below to help you analyze how you're being seen and how you want to see yourself. Or come up with questions of your own—as long as they're open-ended and inwardly directed. It's better to ask, *How can I bring my best qualities out into the world?* than *Will I ever get famous?*

- Am I recognized for what I do best?

- Do I have hidden talents that aren't being fully expressed?

- Am I passed over for promotions and special assignments, or am I acknowledged for my work?

- Does my boss, spouse, or partner seem to take me for granted?

- How would my friends (family, co-workers, spouse, partner) describe me?

- What would they say about my character?

- How would I like to be remembered? Do I have a clear idea of the legacy I want to leave to the world?

- What steps am I taking to leave a meaningful legacy?

Your answers to these questions, or your own questions, become a sort of checklist you can use to work with the inner wisdom of Fame and Reputation. If you're not recognized for what you do best, how can you stop hiding your light under a bushel? If you think that your friends might give you a less than stellar rating in some area or other, what actions can you take to align your behavior with the *you* that you want the world to see?

Love, Marriage & Relationships

"Receptive Earth"

Core concepts: Receptivity, self-love, compassion, romance, connection, passion, loving kindness, partnership

Personal practice: Cultivate your inner magnetism to draw in and keep relationships.

Soul qualities: An open mind, always coming from a place of love

Vital lesson: Love grows from the inside out.

Colors: Reds, pinks, whites

Enhancements: Artwork, symbols, and quotes representing love and compassion. Pairs of accessories.

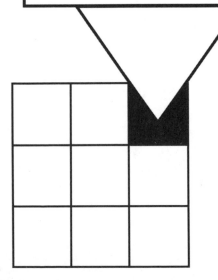

CHAPTER 8

OPENING THE HEART

The Love, Marriage, and Relationships Gua

The spaces between your fingers were created so that another's could fill them in.

— ANONYMOUS

My client Sharyn was beautiful, personable, talented, and successful in her sports marketing career—yet one important dream eluded her. At the age of 45, she had yet to find the man she wanted as her life partner, though she'd searched for many years. "It's like Charlotte says in *Sex and the City*," she told me wryly. "I've been dating since I was 15. Where is he?"

Sharyn was a bit skeptical of feng shui when she called me for a consultation, but she couldn't claim that her other strategies were all that successful! She had no trouble meeting people or getting along with them, and she had tried all the conventional avenues: socializing with friends, friends recommending friends, Internet dating sites, and so on. She knew she needed to try a new approach to generate some positive activity in her love life.

When I stepped into her comfortable, elegant Colonial-style home with its eclectic mix of furniture and décor, it didn't take long to see where the problems lay. Sharyn's home scene, not unlike Jeff's, was anchoring an explicit point of view, that of a single gal. She would need to focus on her physical environment, redirect the energy to visually support her romantic intentions and enhance the Love, Marriage, and Relationships gua of her home.

Though Sharyn's bedroom, located in the Wealth and Prosperity area of the Bagua, was beautifully decorated—spare and uncluttered, in soft blue and neutral gray—it was a room designed for one person, not two. This is typical when you live alone, as you tend to acquire furnishings, accessories, and décor suitable for the single life. For example, heaps of cushions on the bed, no matter how decorative, signal outwardly that the bed is already taken—and Sharyn's bed was stacked with bolsters and accent pillows three deep. With the master bedroom located in the Wealth and Prosperity corner, one would expect Sharyn to have an abundance of suitors! However, the room lacked the symbolic images and gestures that would indicate that a couple dwelt there.

"Does this room look romantic to you?" I asked.

"No," she admitted, and laughed.

To transform the setting, I suggested she give the room a thorough cleaning to eliminate stagnant energy, then remove many of the books (which signal that the occupant will be reading in bed, not focused on a partner) and family photographs (which shift the emphasis away from a couple's relationship). After that, she could start to turn the bedroom into a romantic retreat. My first recommendation always involves the bedspread, because it's the focal point of the room and can either invite you in or push you away. For Sharyn's room, I also recommended that she adjust the color palette by bringing in warmer hues; cool colors such as blues and greens are calm and soothing, whereas warm colors "ignite" a space with passion. Lighting has a powerful effect on mood, so I suggested either three-way lamps or a dimmer that would let her turn the lights down gradually before bedtime, shifting the bright Yang energy toward softer Yin and giving the room the visual appeal of a cozy, sensual space.

In the master bath attached to the bedroom—another significant space that a couple shares—the feeling remained fairly sterile. I suggested that Sharyn extend the bedroom's new color scheme into this room as well, using even deeper hues on the walls to counteract the white fixtures and light-colored tile floor. On a blank wall over her sunken bathtub, I recommended that she hang a reproduction of a painting I love, *The Kiss* by Gustav Klimt, which is an iconic image of a woman embraced by her lover—a stirring yet harmonious picture of adoring intimacy. Sharyn could enhance the new romantic tone of the setting still further with soft lighting (another dimmer), candles around the bathtub, sensuously soft towels, and even an accent lamp on the vanity if space permitted.

Next I asked to see the Love, Marriage, and Relationships gua. In Sharyn's floor plan, this area was occupied by the guest bedroom. As we walked toward it, my eye was drawn to a large photograph on the wall beside the door. I gasped! Janis Joplin was hanging prominently at the entrance to the Love gua, with an accent light illuminating her. Any time you add light, it empowers the image with even greater energy, like a power boost.

"Don't you like Janis Joplin?" Sharyn asked, seeing my expression.

"It's a great picture," I said. "But she was a drug addict and an alcoholic, she was single, and she's dead. We need to move her to a different space. Instead, let's find a piece of artwork that better reflects Love and Marriage to hang on this wall that will serve as a greeter when you enter the room." I suggested, as an example, something by artist Bill Brauer, known nationally for his sensual, yet beautifully rendered figurative paintings. When you want to accelerate the energy, strong visual examples are the most effective.

As we moved through the house, I shared with Sharyn my feng shui philosophy of romance. The choices we make in décor and the images we surround ourselves with in artwork and accessories mirror our mind-set about relationships and love. This visual energy becomes deeply anchored in the home environment and embedded in the consciousness—and inevitably it expands outward. Even after we walk out the front door, we bring those attitudes to bear on interactions with everyone we meet, consciously or not. Sharyn's home was weighing her down with implicit, yet powerful, suggestions that love was doomed to fail and there was no room in her life for a relationship anyway. She wasn't likely to have much luck meeting "the one" if she carried that energy with her on a date!

Just as important as her physical environment, I told Sharyn, was her internal feng shui. If she could examine her beliefs about relationships from the inside out, she could come to see that her authentic self was unique and desirable and that she didn't need external validation to measure her self-worth. She could attract a partner just as she was, complete with her imperfections, without losing herself in the process. Rather than feeling compelled to scan every social gathering for some imaginary perfect match, she could draw into her life a mate who mirrored her qualities and values—a true and lasting love.

I left Sharyn that day with a complete game plan for the redesign of her physical environment *and* her internal landscape. She set about redecorating her home in ways that would help her stay clear about what love and romance meant to her, thereby ensuring that she was sending romantic signals out into the world as well—without attempting changes that were too costly or inconvenient to happily carry out. She made a shopping trip to pick up some new artwork—focusing on images that spoke to *her* of the excitement and mystery of love and the deep desire to connect with another, whatever those images happened to be—and accents in her new, warm color palette, such as a red vase to replace a blue one. The bed got a new bedspread with simple accent pillows, leaving ample welcoming space for a partner; the photo of Janis Joplin was relocated to the dining room, where it became an excellent conversation piece.

Ten weeks later, on Match.com, Sharyn met Larry. They were the same age, with the same values and goals. One year to the day after they moved in together, Larry proposed. Larry didn't quite understand what feng shui was about, yet he was drawn to Sharyn's romantic décor and felt immediately comfortable in her home. They invited me to the wedding, because Larry said, "We have to have the feng shui lady there." He was not leaving anything to chance!

WORKING WITH LOVE, MARRIAGE, AND RELATIONSHIPS

For me, there is no life aspect in the Bagua that is more important than Love, Marriage, and Relationships. This is because connecting with people on a deep level—whether friends, business associates, family members, or romantic partners—is essential to aligning with your own pure potential. Within a deep and connected relationship, we are able to face our fears, admit our jealousies, and reveal our perceived inadequacies. Through others whom we trust and respect, we can get to know our true selves without camouflaging our imperfections.

When I was developing my Inner Wisdom Bagua, working with the *I Ching* to discern the qualities of each gua at the level of inner wisdom, I asked questions that ultimately centered on issues of trust, self-esteem, and fear of the unknown. If I felt that a man I was dating was unreliable, inconsistent, or emotionally distant, I would consult the *I Ching*. Each hexagram in the *I Ching* works as a mirror to the situation at hand and provides a lesson, such as not holding on to timetables set by fears, not listening to the voice of doubt within. It is the way of the *I Ching* that by correcting ourselves, we correct the world around us.

The *I Ching* acts as a lantern to illuminate the truth that everything happens for a good purpose, though that may not be fully understood until later. In relationships, this requires us to remain detached or in a mode of nonaction, not letting ourselves be upset by what happens when people are indifferent, inconsiderate, or unfaithful. Instead, we allow time and space for others to correct themselves without cross-examination or manipulation from us. We engage with another person when moments of awareness and receptivity come around, and we retreat to a neutral attitude in times of darkness. The Love, Marriage, and Relationships gua engages all the aspects of life that involve opening ourselves to others:

receptivity, self-love, compassion, romance, connection, passion, loving kindness, partnership, and an open heart and mind. This gua asks us to cultivate our inner magnetism to draw in and keep relationships. It helps us grow from the inside out.

On the Bagua map, the Love, Marriage, and Relationships gua is found in the rear right corner. You can support this energy by enhancing the gua in your home, on your property, or on a surface such as a desk or dresser top. You can also work on the room that's most strongly connected to romance and relationship—your bedroom—regardless of what gua it occupies in your home. And, of course, you're enhancing the gua whenever you do anything that supports its qualities in your inner life: staying true to yourself by maintaining your identity while you're in close relationships with others, whether they be friends or lovers, and rather than creating a script of what you want in another person, strengthening the qualities that you yourself have to give. If you want to concentrate on dramatically improving your love life, you'll need to enhance the Love, Marriage, and Relationships gua at all these levels, follow a complete and concentrated program for attracting romance and keeping relationships strong.

THE ENERGY OF LOVE

The Love, Marriage, and Relationships gua, in the rear third of your home, is by nature a Yin area, so Yin energy is the one to invite in when you want to give romance a boost. The element most strongly associated with this gua is Fire, which lives in the power area of the Bagua along the back of the home. Fire's color is red, shading across the spectrum from deep purple and burgundy into pink and white on the right side, where Love resides. If you're in a relationship that's already pretty hot—passionate, argumentative, or even volatile—you can dial it down by decorating with those softer, sweeter hues. If the relationship is lacking a spark, on the other hand, you can turn up the temperature with more fiery shades of red, bright and true. Fire energy can also be enhanced with accessories and imagery—some obvious (fireplaces, candles, images of these in artwork) and some less so (images of animals or people, and animal materials such as leather and fur).

As powerful as these classic feng shui considerations are, it's equally important to consider the visual and emotional energy of your environment—the messages that your home is giving you every minute and sending out through you into the world. Single people tend to buy just one of everything—one bedside lamp, one reading chair—and to live, work, and play solo, anchoring solo energy in furniture, artwork, and accessories so their environment reinforces their circumstances (much like Sharyn's picture of Janis Joplin). Single objects are symbolic gestures that anchor single status. If you're single and trying to change your status, take an inventory of your home to see whether it's supporting that goal, and then add a second vase to balance the one that's already on the table or hang a picture that has romantic con-notations—*for you.* It's the intention you assign to every enhancement that creates the real power of feng shui, so the image that gives you the feeling of an open heart may not be the same as anyone else's. I personally like abstract sculptures of two people in-tertwined, giving the impression of an endless con-tinuum of love. This concept can also be reflected in artwork representing pairs of anything, such as two trees, two flowers, or two animals.

WALL-TO-WALL ROMANCE

Many feng shui books, when they talk about romance, focus solely on the Love, Marriage, and Relationships corner of your floor plan, no matter what room occupies that space. Of course, you have to work with what you have! Even if the gua is an office, a bathroom, or a garage, you can bring an element of romance and relationship into the space in whatever way is appropriate for its purpose, using the enhancements we've just discussed: pairs of ob-jects, Yin décor and fire colors, artwork that reso-nates romantically for you. However, it's also wise to enhance romantic energy in all your Love corners: in every gua and every room of your home, the property your home sits on, and even the surfaces within each room. You find the Love corner by ap-plying the Bagua map to a room, or a surface such as a desktop, just as you apply it to your whole floor plan, aligning the bottom of the Bagua with the front edge of the surface or the wall that contains the door to the room. In this corner, you can place photos of you and a loved one, friend, or family member capturing a joyous moment; a vase of fresh flowers (the visual implication is that you're not waiting for someone to *bring* you flowers); or a keepsake box filled with loving notes you've received from others. If you have outdoor space, you can enhance the Love corner of your yard or patio by making sure the space is designed for two people; for example, a bench or two chairs facing in the same direction can suggest a couple looking at life together with a shared point of view. Sculptures are also a good choice: the traditional mandarin ducks, a pair of lovebirds, or anything that represents pairs or peace for you.

It's particularly important to maximize this energy in your master bedroom, which is a crucial room for relationships, no matter what gua it's in. As I mentioned in the previous chapter, my master bedroom is in the Fame and Reputation area of my house. But because of the importance of this room, I decorate it with symbols of coupledom, rather than focusing on the self—displaying diplomas, awards, and so on would detract from the relational energy that a bedroom needs. I save my diplomas and certificates for my office walls and the Fame and Reputation areas of other rooms in my home.

Master bedrooms should look and feel romantic while at the same time promoting relaxation and rejuvenation. The goal is to create a sensual sanctuary for adults, so photos of children and other family members are more suitable in other rooms. Cherubs, while some consider them romantic symbols, are modeled on children, so they should be placed elsewhere as well. As I mentioned at the start of this chapter, you'll often see a bed piled with soft pillows in beautiful fabrics—another look that many people imagine to be romantic—but no matter how luxurious the image, the symbolic message it sends is *This space is occupied.* If you want to attract a mate, it's a good idea to leave him or her some room on the mattress.

And if your goal is to spend time with this mate in a romantic setting at the end of your day, please consider relocating your TV to another room. Otherwise you may find your partner too wrapped up in watching the news to connect with you. If you can't bear to go into your bedroom without turning the TV on, put it in an armoire with doors that you can close, or drape a scarf or a throw over it before you go to sleep. Ask yourself if you're creating an atmosphere designed to draw in your potential mate or if you're cultivating a long-term relationship with the television!

Naturally, a master bedroom is an ideal use for the Love, Marriage, and Relationships gua, something to keep in mind if you're choosing or building a new home or have the ability to repurpose the space you're in now. A guest room, porch, or lanai would be suitable as well. It's best to avoid using this gua as an office—which is best used by one person alone—or as a master bathroom, unless you enhance it properly. But if that is your situation, the office should have visible objects representing pairs, such as two guest chairs, artwork with paired images (they needn't be romantic images—two sailboats would be fine), and warm colors. If it's a master bathroom, you can still choose romantic décor, as I suggested for Sharyn—and be sure to keep the toilet seats down and sink and tub stoppers closed to avoid having relationships go down the drain. If the space happens to be a workout room, make sure that it's designed to accommodate two and that you use it with your partner on a regular basis, in the spirit of advancing your mutual interest in good health and vitality.

If your Love, Marriage, and Relationships gua is in the kitchen, then having a table for two and dining at it regularly, even if you're alone or with a friend rather than a love interest, keeps the energy moving in the right direction. Dining alone in front of the TV is setting up a single existence. Creating culinary delights for yourself and others gives you practice for future dinner parties and intimate dining experiences. If the gua is occupied by a wardrobe, storage closet, garage, or any other area that is not part of a living space, be sure keep the area uncluttered, clean, and organized. Clutter communicates that the space is already taken, and how will your mate ever find you in the maze?

Finally, if the layout of your home puts the Love gua out of your control—perhaps a neighboring apartment or a neighbor's property line juts into that corner—you can still honor love with enhancements to the walls that border the gua. It's also important to activate the Love, Marriage, and relationships corner of all the other rooms in the house.

LOVE AND YOUR LIFE PURPOSE

All the guas play a part in aligning you with your legacy, and they all need to be brought into balance, but you have to start somewhere—at the point that's most important for you. For Sharyn, the starting point was love and her deep desire for a relationship with a partner. For someone else, it might be a relationship of a different kind. The Love, Marriage, and Relationships gua focuses on the quality of relationships you build with co-workers, love interests, family members, and even with yourself. The pairs of objects that enhance this energy—two lamps, two bookends—symbolize links, as in a chain, which lend strength, and your own strength to weather challenging times is doubled by reliable and stable connections. I believe that the quality of your life is deeply based on your relationships and almost all things—especially people—are stronger in tandem.

You'll hear a lot of talk about finding your "soul mate," the kind of talk that Sharyn had bought into with her belief that she had to find that one perfect partner. Actually, I do believe there is someone out there who is ideal for each of us—a true love, a gift from the Universe. However, searching for this other half as a way to feel whole is exhausting. To be constantly on the lookout for that one person, the one you think you will change the quality of your life forever, only keeps you feeling incomplete and perpetuates a sense of desperation. The truth is, the Universe would never create your ideal mate without also giving you the ability to find him or her!

So why not widen the perspective to include the prospect of *everyone* being a soul mate? By those lights, every person who comes into our lives, whether by choice or circumstance, is a teacher of sorts, each encounter and experience a source of insight to help us grow. They expose character flaws to be addressed, bringing us that much closer to reaching our full potential. Each relationship reveals what we need to work on, and what we resist persists.

What I call "universal soul mate energy" draws out in us the attributes that ultimately attract romantic relationships. Whether we're interacting with a friend, a relative, or someone we barely know, being compassionate, accepting, and loving with everyone strengthens the character. Making every effort to be our best, we connect at a more evolved level and avoid slipping back into old patterns that lead to failed relationships. If you're truly ready for a relationship, you can improve the odds by eliminating negative self-dialogue, such as *I don't want to risk getting hurt again* or *No one is worth the pain* or *I'm not in a place where I can care about anyone but me.* Keeping your heart in lockdown is a surefire way to guarantee a nonexistent love life.

Hiding from the possibility of a relationship solely because you're afraid of being hurt will prevent you from having the opportunity to feel the joy of admiration from others.

I'm speaking from experience here. I have been divorced since 1983. In 2007, I wrote a letter inviting my ideal man into my life. I based my definition of "ideal" on the way he made me feel, not what he looked like or could do for me financially. I was very precise, and the letter was loaded with examples of how this man would make me feel: loved, safe, secure. He would comfort me when my parents passed, and he would become my family of choice. With him, I wouldn't be worried about saying the right thing or hiding my vulnerability. I could be heard, without responding in a critical voice, and I could be fully myself. The letter was in the present tense, to give it the energy of an immediate reality rather than a far-off future: *He gives me roots and wings,* I wrote, meaning both the security of a loving environment and the freedom to pursue my dreams and aspirations. *I no longer feel anxious, restless, or sad. I have always wanted to feel cherished, and now I do.*

Then I placed the letter in a box and let go. I decided to have faith in my future and not always be watching with my inner eye to monitor its progress. Whenever I found myself doubting, I would reread the letter to make sure it was what I ultimately wanted. I would ask myself, *Will it be worth the wait if it's the ideal person for me?* You can ask this—*Will it be worth the wait?*—about anything at all that you want in life. For me, the answer was always yes. I trusted in divine timing, knowing that it might take a while for people, places, and circumstances to line up. And they did—in February 2010, three years later, when a man showed up who hadn't been available in 2007.

When a relationship prospect appears, that's the moment when the real work begins. To ensure that the person is genuinely your true love and that the relationship is undeniably in your highest good, you must use the time-proven principles of feng shui.

CHOOSING TO BE CHERISHED

When you honor your own interests, go all out to build loving and lasting relationships with family and friends, and remain faithful to your own unique path in life, you are connected to your true self—and your true self becomes your own personal GPS for drawing in and keeping your true love. Just as there are four seasons in nature, each revealing itself in turn, over time people will reveal everything about themselves, good and bad. This is how you determine whether you are compatible with someone: you have to find out who they are and, as they reveal themselves, believe them. So begin any new relationship with friendship. Getting to know someone slowly is the feng shui way to build a foundation based in reality.

Your goal is to have common ground on key aspects of life, and open and clear conversation with a potential mate is an opportunity to cover this ground—to exchange life and career goals, moral and ethical philosophies, and personal interests that feed your soul. Revealing what is essential to your spirit opens a space for a relationship to go beyond mutual attraction and surface qualities. Silencing your feelings for fear of rejection is rooted in insecurity; a partner will respect you more if you are willing to stand up for yourself and not come across as needy, dependent, or easily manipulated. And if he or she doesn't run from your honesty, you're on the right track.

Other essentials of a true love connection aligned with feng shui principles include trust, mutual respect, patience, humility, and forgiveness. We've all been in situations where we've met someone and given our unquestioned trust right away, only to be disappointed by the other person's actions. Trust is crucial to love, and it takes time to build.

At the same time, there ought to be a natural exchange of affection, respect, and admiration. If one is holding back, the other feels the imbalance. No one should patiently endure another's insensitivity, immaturity, or emotional distance. But we have to refrain from trying to manipulate or influence a situation's outcome. It's an illusion to think we have to micromanage a relationship for it to work. Giving the other person space to meet us halfway—to step willingly into a place of harmony—is the way of feng shui.

SELF-INQUIRY: LOVE, MARRIAGE, AND RELATIONSHIPS FROM THE INSIDE OUT

When I widened my focus from finding "the one" to considering everyone as a soul mate, it became much easier for me to cultivate soul mate qualities in myself. By focusing on attributes such as compassion, understanding, creativity, and integrity, I gave myself a greater chance of attracting someone who mirrored these qualities than if I had been out searching for "the one" with no game plan.

To make the shift, I had to take a hard look at myself to see if I embodied the personal values of good feng shui, including compassion, trustworthiness, receptivity, integrity, modesty, and an open mind. I had to be willing to form strong, mutually beneficial connections with others based on chemistry, consistency, compatibility, clear communication, and common ground. I asked myself if I could improve on any of the personal qualities, such as compassion and self-esteem. I also inquired if I could do a better job of forming and maintaining friendships, family relations, and ultimately a love interest, by being my authentic self, not masking myself to please others at any cost. Rather than hiding my imperfections, I would commit to presenting myself as I was, a work in progress, willing to grow and evolve.

You can do the same thing to examine your outlook on love and relationships. Use the questions below—or questions of your own—to kick your intuition into gear.

- Do I have a good self-image? If not, what needs to change?

- If I'm single, do I enjoy a meaningful social life?

- Do I yearn for a loving relationship, yet can't find the right person?

- Is there anything in my character or personality that people find unpleasant?

- In a romantic relationship, do I ever feel isolated or estranged?

- Does my partner keep me at an emotional distance?

- Do I find it difficult to be vulnerable with my partner?

- What steps am I taking to develop friendships and reliable connections with others?

Remember to keep your questions focused more on what's going on within than without. *How long will it take to meet my soul mate? Why doesn't this guy I like call me back? Where is the best place to meet someone?* These are not the questions you want to be asking. Rather, if you are working on enhancing your personal qualities and values, you are raising your potential to find a like-minded partner with energy that matches your own—someone you meet as a spiritual equal on common ground.

Health & Family

"Shocking Thunder"

Core concepts: Strength, forgiveness, boundaries, discernment, flexibility, expression, intuition, cooperation, ancestors

Personal practice: Seek optimum physical, mental, emotional, and spiritual health.

Soul qualities: Emphasis on maintaining a strong family and friends of choice

Vital lesson: It's not what you're eating; it's what's eating you.

Colors: Blues, greens

Enhancements: Quotes of honesty and forgiveness, family photos, healthy plants, and artwork of gardens and landscapes.

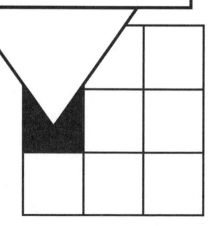

CHAPTER 9

BUILDING STRONG SUPPORT

The Health and Family Gua

Boundaries are to protect life,
not to limit pleasures.

— EDWIN LOUIS COLE

"I feel like my body is breaking down," my long-time client Julie said on the phone. I was surprised, because I knew that Julie was an outdoor enthusiast who enjoyed an active exercise regimen that kept her healthy and fit. What was going on? She wondered the same thing as she explained to me that in addition to aches and pains that were becoming constant, she thought she might have some sort of chronic muscle pull in her leg. Already very knowledgeable about feng shui, Julie felt she could use a tune-up with a second pair of feng shui eyes to help her identify the trouble spots.

After a general tour of Julie's home to get a sense of any energy weaknesses, my first stop to explore further was the Health and Family gua. Nothing seemed out of place. So I went to investigate other areas of the home that might point to the deficiency of energy linked to her health issues. I noticed that she had a beautiful garden area in her screened lanai, but several of the plants were either dead or dying. "What is going on with your garden?" I asked her.

She replied, "I love to tinker in my garden and I haven't had any time. It makes me depressed just to look at the condition of my plants."

"Why haven't you made time for something that brings you so much joy?"

"My boyfriend is constantly on the go with sports and exercise," she said, "and he wants me to be with him."

That made sense to me, since I knew Julie's boyfriend, Steve, was a real exercise fanatic. Whereas Julie balanced her fitness routine with yoga, meditation, and walks on the beach, Steve's restless energy made him easily bored—if he wasn't moving, he wasn't happy. Noting that the lanai was in the Love, Marriage, and Relationships gua of Julie's home, I asked, "And how is your relationship going?"

"I'm beginning to resent him for my having to be jumping, running, hiking, and biking every free minute we have together, and my body is complaining!"

These three critical pieces of information—her health concerns, the state of the lanai garden, and the resentment that was building in the relationship with her boyfriend—alerted me to the areas of the Bagua map that were causing Julie's frustration and therefore depleting her energy level. I knew that the inner wisdom of feng shui in the Health and Family gua would come into play for Julie, since one of the great lessons of this gua has to do with supporting ourselves by establishing boundaries.

We talked about how important it was to maintain Yin and Yang energy in balance, and I said I thought her body was trying to communicate with her through the demands of extreme exercise causing muscle fatigue. Her plants were trying to communicate with her visually, letting her know that they needed food, water, and attention to sustain them— the same kind of simple care she needed to give herself. Through our conversation, it became apparent that Julie was reluctant to set boundaries with Steve and back away from his obsession with exercise, for fear he'd find another woman who would take her place. I explained that the value of setting boundaries would be to restore balance and harmony, not only to her health but to the relationship. We talked about how the survival of any relationship is contingent on having some common ground—complementary goals and values—while still allowing you to honor your own interests and activities. With boundaries, I told her, you'll find out for sure if he is willing to invest positive energy in the relationship and honor your wishes. If his energy is easily distracted elsewhere or directed toward someone else after you've communicated your feelings, it's time to find a partner whose path is more aligned with yours.

Julie had a thoughtful and heartfelt conversation with Steve, who met her suggestions with resistance. Even so, she began to balance her own activities, joining him in the gym and outdoor sports sometimes and other times letting him go without her while she tended her garden. She began regular sessions with a physical therapist to locate the source of her body's discomfort and begin the healing process. She bought new plants, repotted some she already had, and rearranged her entire garden setting. She felt happy and less stressed with this slower pace, and she even created a meditation area within her Zen garden where she could spend restful time by herself.

After two weeks, Steve announced that he was breaking off the relationship because he needed his "space." You might cringe at hearing that this particular feng shui consultation resulted in the dissolution of a relationship—how is that a good thing? Julie was the first to say it was a gift. She found out that Steve had met another woman who was an avid hiker and would willingly indulge his extreme need for exercise. In addition, after several months of physical therapy, the therapist traced the source of

Julie's chronic pain and feeling of a perpetual pulled muscle in her leg to an uneven muscular structure resulting from an old car accident. The extreme exercising had flushed out this hidden injury that would eventually have caught up with her anyway. With her body alignment restored to full health and joyfully tending to her garden of "relationships," Julie felt a new source of strong support, and she felt blessed to have realized that seeking happiness outside herself through Steve had left her feeling empty and disconnected.

WORKING WITH HEALTH AND FAMILY

The last gua we worked on was all about relating to others in the context of coupledom and partnership; this one looks at relationships from a different angle, examining and enhancing the network of family and friends that surrounds you and supports you in difficult times. It also takes into account the support you give yourself by tending to all aspects of your own well-being—your physical, mental, emotional, and spiritual health.

The Health and Family gua, located in the left center square of the Bagua map, lends itself to use as a family room, child's bedroom, office, bathroom, or kitchen. (Of course, as we've seen, no matter what room it is, you can still activate its energy with intelligent enhancements.) In this middle zone between the front and the back of a building, Yin and Yang have equal influence, so the décor of a room should reflect that harmony—neither suffused with soft Yin finishes nor dominated by bright, hard Yang flourishes. Since this gua is all about boundaries, the inner wisdom of Yin and Yang here has to do with balancing connection and self-containment so that relationships with family and friends stay harmonious.

The element associated with this gua is Wood, which supports us in being flexible, cooperative, and forward-thinking. You can bring the energy of Wood into your environment through living plants (all the more reason for Julie to cultivate her garden), wooden furniture, floral prints (especially in fabrics like cotton and rayon), or images of landscapes. Stripes, beams, pillars, and columns all invite Wood into a space, as do the colors green and blue.

To further promote good health and dependable relationships within your family (or your family of friends), traditional enhancements to your outer environment include photos of loved ones on truly happy occasions; healthy plants and fresh flowers; and inspirational quotes about honesty, friendship, gratitude, or forgiveness. Feng shui don'ts for this gua include spiky plants such as cactus (you don't want prickly relationships!), dead or dying plants, or anything like potpourri (more dead energy). To enhance this gua from within, tend to your health in every way you can, starting with healthy eating and regular exercise. Work to expand your character attributes of flexibility, sincerity, and understanding and to set boundaries with family and friends to help ensure that everyone learns to honor the decisions that are best for their respective lives.

ESSENTIAL BOUNDARIES

Lately it seems you can't pick up a self-help, spirituality, or relationship book that doesn't mention "unconditional love" as the favored method of loving others, regardless of anything they do or don't do. This implies that there are only two choices: loving someone with conditions and loving someone without conditions. In the feng shui philosophy, it's not either/or: the essence of love is pure, free, and selfless, *and* it requires boundaries to thrive.

Boundaries are crucial to deflecting negative energy. Since feng shui takes its cues from nature, including the animal kingdom, we can look at the armor on an armadillo's back as a symbol of boundaries. An armadillo can shield itself by rolling into a ball that its enemies can't penetrate. Without such a shield, you're like a sponge, absorbing negativity and criticism from loved ones, taking on their moods and emotional baggage or allowing *them* to take *you* for granted, depleting your essential energy. When you set boundaries, you're laying down guidelines for what you are willing to experience and what you aren't—and what you experience is in your control, not visited on you against your will. Boundaries in relationships mean that there are certain things you will tolerate and certain things you won't. They're different for every person and for every relationship.

I use a traditional Native American medicine wheel as a visual reminder to maintain boundaries in my life. It's hanging on my bathroom mirror, in the form of a dream catcher, so that I see it every day.

The medicine wheel is made of two circles, one inside the other, held together by a web that stretches between them. I think of the center of the medicine wheel as my Earth center—a place of harmony and peaceful living. The web represents all the positive experiences and people I want in my life—all that bring me joy. The outer circle rim is my boundary; outside it are the people and experiences I wish to keep at a respectful distance. It's a shield, deflecting energy I don't want in my life. It's not meant to hide behind out of fear; acting from fear or insecurity keeps you from feeling the admiration of others in a positive way. It simply gives me an opportunity to act as my own gatekeeper and accept or reject situations as they come.

Your intuition is the key to making those choices—what to let in, what to keep at a distance. On the intuitive plane, you tap into a level of consciousness where more information is available to you than you normally know, and it can be your best guide in determining how to react to and interact with people around you. If you try to control every life experience by making up your mind about it ahead of time, you hinder the intuitive process; conversely, you can accelerate the process if you're willing to give up your attachment to being right. And letting go of being right opens up new possibilities for resolving conflicts and making decisions: as you scrutinize the facts before you, you rely on your inner knowing to skillfully guide you to what's right for you.

Forgiveness enhances intuition by freeing you from dwelling on past events. If you harbor even a drop of anger, resentment, or bitterness about something that's past, you stay stuck with that feeling, a prisoner in your own jail. Forgiveness doesn't require you to excuse a terrible injustice or let people get away with serious misdeeds, and it doesn't mean pretending that everything is all right between you. Many times, both parties are hurt deeply; reconciliation is not always the desired result. And you don't necessarily have to make personal contact with someone to forgive or at least begin the process of forgiveness; just refrain from speaking ill of the person, and if you have nothing good to say, say nothing at all. Think of it this way: since no one is perfect, you can be sure there will be (and have been) times when you need someone's compassionate forgiveness for your own missteps. Even if there's no chance of renewing a relationship, you can choose to forgive a person— or even an experience—by letting go of your wish that the past be different.

Self-Inquiry: Health and Family from the Inside Out

How strong is your system of support? How firm are your boundaries—and are they placed to serve you well, protecting without keeping out what you *do* want to receive from the world around you? Ask yourself these questions, or others of your own devising, to access the inner wisdom of the Health and Family gua.

- Do I have stable relationships with family members and friends?

- Can I rely on my friends and family when I need help?

- Do I feel the need to seek spiritual nourishment?

- Am I suffering from chronic pain?

- Do I take it very much to heart when someone criticizes me?

- Do I tend to mirror other people's moods or feel their pain?

- Is there any event or situation from the past that I'm holding on to, anything that may be preventing me from enjoying a happy present and a hopeful future?

- Could my social life and circle of supportive friends improve in any way?

- Am I experiencing chronic pain that prevents me from participating in day-to-day activities or accepting social invitations?

Depending on the insights these questions bring up, you may find that you need to examine the circles you're drawing in your life to invite in more of what you want and more effectively keep out what you don't. How can you get the support you need to cultivate *your* garden?

Creativity & Children

"Joyous Lake"

Core concepts: Joy, creativity, focus, logic, encouragement, imagination, originality

Personal practice: Laugh, dance, create, paint, sing, play.

Soul qualities: Joy from within, passion that creates discipline; willingness to nurture your inner child

Vital lesson: Dream with your eyes open.

Colors: White, pastels

Enhancements: Quotes and artwork of children, joy, and creativity. Display of creative projects and hobbies.

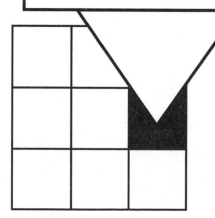

CHAPTER 10

JOYFUL PLAY

The Creativity and Children Gua

Behold the turtle. He only makes progress when he sticks his neck out.

— JAMES BRYANT CONANT, FORMER PRESIDENT OF HARVARD UNIVERSITY

For most of my adult life, I wanted to take watercolor painting classes. As a child, my toys of choice were paint-by-number kits and coloring books with crayons. With a busy corporate career, however, I never had time to pursue creative interests, and my definition of expressing creativity was usually coming up with new business ideas.

After I left my corporate life, I looked at the Creativity and Children gua and said to myself, "Now, how are you going to enhance this gua in your home?" The "children" aspect of this gua isn't just literal, it's also about joy, reminding us how children love play and have fun with complete abandon. So, remembering my long-deferred dream, I figured it was about time to sign up for a watercolor class and see where it went.

The course was six two-hour sessions taught by an award-winning watercolor artist named Colleen Cassidy, who owned her own gallery as well. Her teaching strategy was brilliant. Since we didn't know how to draw or paint, she guided us through the process, and at the end of each class, we had finished a painting. Imagine the joy after the first class when we were able to show our friends and families an actual painting!

When the six weeks were over, Colleen told me that she thought I had potential and wanted to move me to an intermediate class. There I was introduced to so many colors and blending techniques to create new colors that it changed the way I decorated my own home and gave me a whole new palette to recommend to clients in my interior decorating business. This experience directly enhanced my skills as a professional decorator—but more than that, it was nurturing my creative gene.

My watercolor painting evolved, and I hung my creations in my office, which happens to be my Health and Family gua, to anchor my creativity within my business ventures, as well in the kitchen, the site of my Creativity and Children gua. Guests in my home praised my paintings and wanted to buy prints! Soon

I expanded my designs to ceramic tiles and ceramic centerpieces in wooden keepsake boxes, all inspired by the colors, shapes, and symbolic images of the Bagua map. I applied for and received a trademark for my line of original designs and now market them under the brand name Living Art®.

As a result of my experiment with taking watercolor lessons, I'm now an award-winning artist with my work sold in three fine art galleries as well as on my website. I'm able to support my feng shui work by creating art and accessories specific to the concepts of each gua in the Bagua map—all because I honored that long-held desire to have some fun!

WORKING WITH CREATIVITY AND CHILDREN

Like all the areas of the Bagua map, the Creativity and Children gua works on both a literal and a symbolic level. If you have children or hope to in the future, this is the gua to enhance to support their positive, healthy, joyful growth. One obvious enhancement is pictures of the children themselves! Of course, the theory of visual energy calls for images symbolic of what you want to achieve, so if you don't have children, you could place photos of yourself with friends' children, photos of nieces and nephews, or artwork of children at play. Since this gua is very much about play, it's the natural joy that children take in life that you want to capture, so use any strong and happy images that draw that energy to you. If there are children in the house, you can put their bedroom in this area; you can also encourage their natural creativity by establishing a set time in the day that includes arts and crafts, dramatic play, science, and nature. Whether you use different rooms for these different activities or combine them all in one space, it's important to honor a child's natural inclination to explore interests and release energy.

Even if you don't have images of children (or actual children), and you simply make this area a craft room that you enjoy, you're embodying the essence of children and creativity. This gua is an important source of nurturing for your *inner* child, if you'll pardon the expression, associated with endeavors that boost the creative process yet still allow you to have fun along the way. Business executives, managers on the home front, parents, and caregivers of all kinds have long lists of responsibilities that require focus and logic. This concentrated attention needs to be balanced with opportunities to set your imagination free in a playful environment—times when you can think and explore outside the box. Whatever stirs your soul and ignites your creative expression will bring you joy: that's the principle at work here in the "play area" of the Bagua.

The Creativity and Children gua, located in the center right third of the Bagua map, is the place to let your decorating genius run free! Décor is, essentially, all about creativity anyway, and this gua asks you to bring creative expression front and center. If you've created your own artwork, place or hang it here, or use accessories and images that relate to a hobby you love or a piece of whimsy that inspires and delights you. From an energetic point of view, although this gua should contain Yin and Yang in harmonious balance, just like the Health and Family gua, you can actually push the Yang quality of experimentation a bit here. With those coloring books and paint-by-number kits, you were always supposed to stay inside the lines; coloring outside the lines was considered a mistake. In my watercolor class, one of my first assignments was to do an abstract painting, but that ran so counter to childhood training that I couldn't think of a thing to do. The teacher said, "Just throw some paint on the paper and see where it goes." That abstract piece is now my best-selling watercolor print!

In addition to a bedroom or playroom for children, this gua makes a good guest bedroom or hobby room; it might be suitable for a home office if you're looking for a balance between work and play in your life. You can enhance this area externally with your own works of art, craft, or writing, as well as photos of yourself as a child at happy times. In this area of my home, in addition to my watercolors, I display a black-and-white photo of me as a small child with my parents, who were very young, in front of our first snow. Our town in California never had snow! It was a childlike moment for all of us. I also have photos up of my parents as children, capturing happy moments for them. To enhance this area from within, you can cultivate the qualities in yourself that support any creative endeavor—imagination, originality, focus, and the discipline that comes from pursuing a passion— and fine-tune all your senses to create a "comfort zone" in your home where creativity can flourish.

ACCESSING CREATIVITY THROUGH THE SIX SENSES

The creative spirit is the energy source needed to reach our full potential, and it's the essence of inner joy. Once you have activated your creative capability, your inner satisfaction for life never runs dry, no matter what is happening in your life. Creative people invent, problem-solve, and communicate in new ways. They have no need to "think outside the box," because for them there is no box. The seeds of creativity reside in every one of us, and creativity is essential to how you skillfully approach, act, or react to new circumstances.

Creativity is like a muscle, in that the more you use it, the stronger it gets. Highly creative people embody the traits of courage, flexibility, motivation, and intuition in order to expand the boundaries of what is possible. For those who want to increase creativity, the six senses are a great place to begin. Paying attention to them increases your ability to be in the present moment. Use some of the suggestions below to enhance your connection to the senses:

Touch: Choose gentle, luxurious fabrics for your furniture, bed linens, and clothing. Not only do they feel soft against your skin, they instantly bring comfort and relaxation to a tired body. Make sure your furniture is supporting you, literally: your mattress, your office chair, or the sofa you curl up on to watch TV shouldn't leave your muscles cramped or your back strained. Over time, holding an uncomfortable position will lead to aggravation and pain that affect your health and may even require a doctor's care.

Smell: The sense of smell is one of our most powerful connections to past memories and present moods. Scents in your home can trigger fond recollections and define what feels like "home" to you—and using scent can be as simple as baking a batch of cookies or lighting a candle with your favorite fragrance. When cleaning, avoid products that leave surfaces smelling sanitized; instead, use natural, nontoxic products with pleasant scents such as lemon or lavender. Fresh herbs growing in your kitchen or in your garden can motivate you to cook a gourmet meal for your family or for guests. Fresh flowers or any form of aromatherapy in your entryway negate any staleness in the setting and bring delight the moment you step inside. Realtors know the magic scent can make: they'll often place a pan of sugar and water sprinkled with cinnamon in a low oven before an open house to give potential buyers an almost subliminal sense of entering a home that's comfortable and warm.

Taste: Taste, in the literal sense, influences many of our choices and habits, whether it's the toothpaste we use or the kinds of snacks we eat. Sitting in a quiet environment for a meal—away from the

TV—is an important first step to truly tasting and consciously enjoying your food. Preparing meals with fresh ingredients, herbs, and spices can make a big difference in the way you eat—and the amount you eat just to feel satisfied. With each bite, pay attention to the food's flavor, texture, and aroma to help curb the tendency to shove food into your body to feel full. This aspect of feng shui is all about taking a creative approach to a better way of life; for some, there's an additional benefit when they find joyful, creative expression in preparing food for family and friends.

Sight: You already know from what you've read so far that visual energy has a profound impact on your life in your space. Choices in the colors, textures, shapes, and design elements of your home can either uplift you or wear your energy down. Lighting is a mood booster, especially natural light. Pets also bring in good visual chi: a wagging tail on your beloved pet can make you feel loved in return, or you can be mesmerized and calmed by watching exotic fish swimming in a tank. Photos displayed around your home can anchor fond memories of vacations, family visits, and faraway friends. A home that is organized, uncluttered, and spacious gives you the sensation that you have plenty of free time to pursue your passions.

Intuition: Using your sixth sense—listening to your gut, following your hunches—gives you a powerful, soulful alternative to logic and reason as a guidance system for your life. And just as you build muscles by lifting weights, you build your intuition through practice. The concept is that you hold all the answers to your questions, and gathering intuitive insight tweaks the visible and logical information that's already in front of you to help you find your way to the truth.

Creativity requires the power of imagination, and the best way to tackle a deficient imagination is to grow and expand the six senses. But you can also do other simple things, like watching a movie without audio and trying to imagine what the actors are saying. It forces you to create a story in your mind in order to complete the scene by using the creative side of your brain. Filling in the gaps trains your brain to generate original thoughts and ideas.

Creative expression can take the form of an activity such as making art, writing, or preparing culinary delights, just to name a few—and it can also mean viewing or presenting something in a unique new way or turning a problem into a positive challenge. *Any* endeavor can be made creative just by approaching it in a way that's different from the status quo, shying away from conventional thinking, or minimizing criticism and censorship—your own as well as others'. Many people claim, "I'm not creative," when the truth is that everyone is creative! Any time you have an idea, then take a step to advance it, creativity expands.

A fully engaged creative spirit will help you see mistakes as lessons, not failures. Disappointments become challenges. Setbacks are merely pauses. Every chaotic situation is an opportunity. You are no longer locked into a pattern of behaving a certain way because you've been told that's the way it's always been done. Your creative spirit will find a new way, perhaps even a better way, to persevere.

MAKING SPACE FOR A CREATIVE SPIRIT

Of course, creativity can only expand if it's got room to grow. I believe the biggest block to creativity is clutter, be it physical clutter in your home or workplace; mental and emotional clutter made up of fixed ideas or inflexible behavior; or spiritual clutter, such as an inability to appreciate that the truth of any situation always lies in the middle or neutral position, the place of harmony.

Clutter is your enemy because it has a purpose! Accumulating clutter keeps you either tethered to the past or distracted by daydreams of the future. It's a destructive cycle, as we saw in Part I: you buy stuff because you feel as if you deserve it, or because it's symbolic of your hard work, or because you think it will somehow make your life easier, or because it makes you feel better to own the same things as your friends, colleagues, or neighbors. But the more you accumulate, the more you become a slave to the process, and it creates more problems than it solves. Clutter makes for stagnation, because energy cannot properly flow into or circulate in a space that's dirty or disorganized. This sluggish energy makes you feel lethargic, unmotivated, and depressed—and how can creativity flourish when you just feel like curling up with a baby blanket and checking out of life?

Clutter can deprive you of your freedom and ultimately of your spiritual self, because it blocks clarity and stifles purpose. You can't very well focus on your hopes and dreams when your spirit is covered in a pile of old newspapers, buried under clothes on the floor, concealed beneath stacks of paper, or swimming amid dirty dishes in the sink. There's good news, though: if you have time to create the clutter, you have time to eliminate it too.

Quick Tips for Clutter Busting: To give your creative juices a jump start, make an appointment with yourself for a decluttering project. It doesn't have to be long—increments of 15 or 30 minutes will work if you can't set aside a couple of hours at a time. You can always extend the time if you get into it, but be gentle with yourself at the start.

Put it into your daily schedule just as you would a doctor's appointment; everyone is capable of keeping a doctor's appointment, and a decluttering date is no different. If you have large-scale clutter to get rid of—furniture or boxes of books—schedule pickups or runs to local charities such as Goodwill. You can also coordinate your decluttering with your weekly trash pickup or plan a yard sale.

Now let's begin!

- Every item must have a home, so plan ahead to house your belongings by buying whatever organizers you need. You can create your own organizers, such as decorative boxes, or buy commercial products. For offices, consider stackable trays for bills or paperwork, and dividers, pocket folders, or hanging files with manila folders for file cabinets.

- Start decluttering in the master bedroom, followed by the entryway to your home, then the rooms you use the most. The goal is to clean, organize, make any necessary repairs, and redecorate a room to completion before you move on.

- Start with a quick sweep. You'll need a trash bag, recycling bins, and empty boxes or storage bins to capture things that don't belong in this room (such as items that belong to other family members) as well as items for charity or sale. Concentrate first on clutter that's on the floor, followed by clutter on surfaces. Remove anything that's hanging on doorknobs or hooks behind doors: doors must open fully, without any restrictions, for maximum energy flow.

- Take out any furnishings, artwork, and accessories that don't fit the function and vision of the room. For example, remove toys from your office and exercise equipment from your bedroom.

- Take everything out of the drawers to open up the space so you can see what needs to get put back in and what can be permanently removed. This is a good time to put organizers in place, before you "stage" the drawer with clothing or other belongings. Place the things you use most in the front and the things you use least in the back. To help you decide what stays or goes, ask questions that will help you make a five-second decision: *Do I love it? Do I need it? Is it functional? Have I used it in the past year?* The faster you make a decision and move on, the more effective your decluttering will be.

You'll find that decluttering in small increments will quickly help you restore order to your home or workplace, making space for creativity to bloom. Make a list of all the things you've wanted to do if only you had the time—and now you do! In my own life, once I really understood the detriment of clutter to the creative process and made decluttering a priority, I found I had the time to pursue my dream of taking watercolor classes.

Self-Inquiry: Creativity from the Inside Out

Does creativity run through a clear channel in your life? How are you making room for joy? Ask yourself the questions below—or other questions that have meaning for you—to access the inner wisdom of the Creativity and Children gua.

- Am I filled with a sense of delight and awe about life?

- Does my future seem bright with possibilities and contentment?

- Do I want to have children? If so, have I had difficulty conceiving?

- Is the work I'm doing balanced with leisure time?

- Do I have a beloved hobby or craft that has taken a backseat in my life?

- If I have children, are they using their natural talents?

- Is there a hidden talent of my own I'd like to pursue?

Use your answers to see if you're trapped in an old pattern and determine whether it's time to take some creative interests, projects, or hobbies off the back burner. And don't forget to have some daily fun!

Knowledge & Self-Cultivation

"Still Mountain"

Core concepts: Quietude, reflection, peace, contemplation, wisdom, meditation, stillness, introspection

Personal practice: Have some daily quiet time.

Soul qualities: Ability to redirect your energy to quieting the monkey mind

Vital lesson: Introspection leads to wisdom.

Colors: Black, blues, greens

Enhancements: Artwork and images of quiet places, mountains, and landscapes. Images of wise and accomplished people. Display of favorite books and affirmations.

CHAPTER 11

GROWING IN WISDOM

The Knowledge and Self-Cultivation Gua

*Self-knowledge is the beginning
of self-improvement*

— SPANISH PROVERB

My client Deb had a number of aspects of her life that needed attention: she hadn't worked in a couple of years, she needed to get her health and fitness regimen in order, and most important to her, she wanted to improve her love life. She had been single since her husband's death 15 years earlier, dating once in a while, but never seriously.

Deb and I sat down to discuss these three aspects of concern, and what we discovered was that underlying all her problems was a change Deb needed to bring about in herself—she needed to learn who she authentically was and how to move in the direction she wanted. To do this, she chose feng shui—both inner and outer—as a way to transform her life. She was opening herself up to a whole body of knowledge—feng shui wisdom—that was new to her.

Immediately, the quote "When the student is ready, the teacher appears" came to my mind. I sensed I was called in as a mentor to introduce her to the key principles of feng shui and empower her to do the work. It was clear that I was there to guide her, but not do the work for her.

We began by looking at the plan for her property. By doing this, I could show her just where she would need to focus her efforts to start her process. Her setup was somewhat challenging: The house was long and narrow, with the garage placed in the center front of the home, in the Career and Life Purpose gua. The Knowledge and Self-Cultivation gua and the Helpful People and Travel gua were outside of her floor plan, part of community property and, therefore, out of her control. Because of this, we discussed that she would have to improve these two guas within the structure of each room to properly represent and support the associated absent energy.

We took a tour of her house and discussed some changes she could implement fairly easily to balance her home's energy. We talked about the importance of applying good feng shui equally throughout her environment, to draw in everything she desired, and we decided that my introduction of the basics would focus on the three specific problems she had outlined, so we began with the Love, Marriage, and Relationships gua. When I walked in, I couldn't help but notice the seven-foot-tall cactus occupying this space. I laughed out loud. "Do you think that means anything?" I asked Deb and then explained that cactus is symbolic of a way to keep people at a distance.

Since she didn't really want to be by herself, we talked about enhancing this area more deliberately, rearranging and selectively reaccessorizing so that the décor of the room reflected pairs of things. And that cactus had to go!

Next was her Career and Life Purpose gua, which would require a twofold approach. She would need to generally declutter and organize her garage to create space and redirect her business ventures to her home office, which was in a nook within the Wealth and Prosperity gua. I suggested expanding a vision board she had started, but arranging the board according to the nine sections of the Bagua map. For example, she could cut out images in magazines that best reflected her career interests and place them in the Career gua of her vision board.

Finally, we looked at her Health and Family gua, which was divided between a staircase to the upper level (a steep climb!) and kitchen cabinets in the adjacent room. Since there wasn't much we could do to the physical environment there, I explained she could really focus on the inner parts of feng shui to jumpstart her health. By initiating a simple walking exercise regimen and paying attention to how certain foods affected her body, then making healthier food choices, she could change the health of this part of her life.

Because this consultation was more about educating her than about having me fix things, we spent a good deal of time talking about the personal practices of Knowledge and Self-Cultivation, including the importance of bringing time for reflection, meditation, and introspection into her life. We set up a plan for her to have some daily quiet time, and I pointed her toward a number of good sources of feng shui information. I left Deb with a feng shui "game plan" and a sense of excitement about how she could transform her life. And she took it and ran. She studied feng shui and implemented its ideas, and it wasn't long before things started to move for her. She got a call from someone she had formerly worked with, telling her about a job that was about to be posted. She applied, as one of 90 qualified candidates, and got the position.

A month later, her neighbor asked her to dinner.

Deb and her son had known Sal for about two years. A retired Marine with a 12-year-old daughter, he was a friendly presence around their apartment complex—they'd see him outside working on his motorcycle, walking the dog, or coming home from one thing or another. When Deb found out he didn't have any space to keep his bike, she told him there was plenty of room in her garage until he figured something else out. She had never really considered having a romantic relationship with him.

Soon he started calling Deb every time he took the bike out or put it away—as a courtesy, he said. Then he started coming to the pool with her and her son. When he asked her out, though, she "kind of freaked out," she told me later. She wasn't looking for a relationship, she was too busy, she had just been back at work for a month, and in her spare time, she was helping her sister and her family through a medical crisis. She tried to blow it off, but eventually she said to herself, *Why not?* So she called Sal and told him that while it was hard for her to get out for dinner, she was usually free for lunch.

So a couple of days later, they went out for lunch. It was nice to get dressed up again, and there wasn't so much pressure. What was funny to Deb was that Sal told *her* how nervous *he* was. He couldn't even finish his lunch.

"Fast-forward to today—he's moving in with us," Deb wrote to me in an e-mail not long afterward. As you can see, the application of feng shui principles can produce many positive and inspiring results!

THE WISDOM WITHIN

All the points on the Inner Wisdom Bagua map direct attention to the space within ourselves as well as without, and the Knowledge and Self-Cultivation gua simply makes this direction explicit. Here is the place where you balance your active life with reflection and introspection. When you need a respite from the noise around you or from your own mental chatter, this gua provides a quiet space where wisdom can take root and your inner voice can make itself heard.

It's almost impossible to overstate the importance of getting quiet and listening within, no matter what it is you're listening for. Stillness clears space in your mind for intuition to thrive. Whenever you're blessed with a steady stream of silence, no matter how brief, you'll think of something you've been meaning to do, or you may get a hit of information you've been seeking. It can be completely unrelated to the task you were just doing. It's an "aha" moment. Therefore, the purposeful scheduling of time for daily reflection is a way to plan a rendezvous with wisdom. This can be accomplished through meditation, sitting quietly with a cup of tea, or blending silently with nature.

As you make a practice of stillness, you may find yourself coming up with innovative ways of doing things through dreams, imagery, thoughts, or feelings. Quiet time restores energy and births new ideas that might not have been available to you before. And anyone who's pursuing some sort of self-development or growth activity, such as going to college or taking extension courses, should pay particular attention to this gua, ideally by creating a space within the home that's suitable for and dedicated to study.

Self-cultivation also means taking care of the needs that are most personal to you. Whenever you take on a role in relation to others—whether as parent, partner, sibling, caretaker, teacher, or friend—you give a piece of yourself to them, and it's important to restore that energy in the way that works best for you: a shopping excursion or a golf outing, a massage or a good laugh, or simply time alone to relax.

The recent trip to Ecuador that I mentioned in Chapter 4 became a wonderful exercise in Knowledge and Self-Cultivation—partly because, before that, I hadn't taken a vacation in seven years. Though I traveled for work throughout my ESPN career, and now travel several times a year to visit and care for my parents, neither of those counts as a vacation! So to restore vitality to my life, I decided to go on this jungle adventure, without any agenda other than to laugh, journal, and take photos that would inspire my watercolor painting. As it turned out, I discovered new interests and old ones that had lain dormant for years. I revived my interest in travel, along with a desire to become fluent in Spanish. I also rediscovered how much I love photography. My work as a producer at ESPN automatically strengthened my ability to create a compelling composition in a snapshot, but I hadn't gotten behind a camera for some time. In Ecuador, I discovered that the organic beauty of the jungle was feng shui at its best. Nature was the author of these unique compositions; my imagination could not create these iconic and innovative images in watercolor art, so why reinvent the original? I'm now planning to buy a new camera, take photography classes, and seek further information and education on travel in South America. This may lead to another component of my feng shui business or just be my "feng shui hobby." What I do know is that knowledge nurtures my soul; from there, I will see what other facets of my full potential emerge.

WORKING WITH KNOWLEDGE AND SELF-CULTIVATION

Knowledge and Self-Cultivation is centered in the front left corner of the Bagua map. Here at the front of the house, where traffic passes in and out (and typically where the house faces a public street), active Yang energy dominates, so it's important to emphasize Yang qualities in the décor of this area, even though its focus is quiet and inwardly directed. Suitable enhancements for this gua include books, educational materials, inspirational quotes, and artwork that represents wisdom, peace, or serene scenes.

The Knowledge and Self-Cultivation gua is a perfect place for an office, study, library, or meditation room; it also makes a good living room or guest bedroom, as long as it's not too noisy outside. However, given its placement in the front left corner, in homes with certain common layouts, this gua often ends up being in the garage, not a room at all. In a garage, obviously, the traditional enhancements of books and inspirational quotes may not work, but you can still enhance the area by keeping it clean and organized, creating a peaceful scene when you drive in. If you can, hang posters on the garage walls that depict places you'd like to visit for a rejuvenating vacation.

What if your Knowledge and Self-Cultivation area is missing altogether—say, part of the driveway? I get asked this all the time, because the floor plan of a house or apartment often isn't a perfect square! In brief, if the area were absent from my home, then not only would I give extra focus to self-cultivation on a regular basis—by journaling, taking classes, or reading books that inspire and instruct—I would also enhance the walls closest to the missing gua, as well as the Knowledge area of each room and each surface in my home. I would specifically hang artwork symbolic of my goals related to wisdom, belief systems, taking care of myself, and seeing my future clearly and peacefully. I might include comfortable chairs on this wall with specific lighting for reading. I might also use books, photos, quotes of inspiration and insight, and accessories that remind me of my personal journey. If I lived in a multi-unit building and the gua included a wall shared with another occupant, I would pay particular attention to enhancements on that wall. When you have a shared wall with another person, there is a tethering effect: what is happening to them may attach to and exert influence over what you are doing. For example, a business might have a wall in its Wealth and Prosperity gua attached to another business that was failing, and it would be important to counteract that influence through intelligent adjustments within the space.

You can develop the qualities of wisdom and inner growth in your daily activities, too, even if they don't take place in this gua. For example, I'm writing right now on my laptop in a chair in my Knowledge and Self-Cultivation area, which creates a clear channel for wisdom to come through. However, I can write from my office, my living room, the public library, or Starbucks, and I'll still be developing the Knowledge and Self-Cultivation area of the Bagua. Reading a book at bedtime, whether in bed or in another room, is working on this gua. The same is true of going in for a massage or a facial or taking a walk on the beach—if it's something that soothes your soul, it's a way to cultivate your self.

THE POWER OF YOUR OWN WORDS

One of the most effective ways to nurture your wisdom and grow your soul is to keep a journal. A written record of your thoughts, experiences, ambitions, dreams, and triumphs captures your state of mind and heart at a certain time in your life, and looking back on it helps you to see how you've learned and grown; your thoughts become more powerful on the page than they are when they're moving through your mind. Over the years, they serve as a barometer for your patterns and habits. Looking back at your journals and contemplating your actions on paper alongside your feelings at that moment helps you sort out the millions of impressions you process in a day, and your insight can keep you from repeating old mistakes in new situations.

There are many reasons to journal besides recording random thoughts. You may want to set goals and track your progress toward them, write down your dreams, note moments of gratitude, track diet and weight loss, record the milestones in your baby's life, or write your autobiography. My favorite journals are hardbound with lined pages; you can use anything you like, of course, from an elegant handmade volume to a simple spiral-bound notebook or legal pad. Label and date the journal on the first page. You may want to write in a favorite quote that relates to the function the journal will serve for you.

It's important to set aside a time to write in your journal that you know will be free of distractions. I always like to start with a small increment, an amount of time I can afford to set aside without feeling pressured by other obligations or getting frustrated with time parameters. I devote 15 minutes with some wiggle time at the end, in case I get on a roll. You can always spare 15 minutes, and once you do so, you'll be able to gauge how much time to you need to make room to journal on a regular basis. To get started, write whatever comes into your mind—don't edit yourself, and don't stop until you run out of material that wants a witness. By expressing everything you're feeling, you give your own voice the opportunity to be heard without any restrictions, whether that means recording the highlights of your week or the accomplishments of your family and friends or your own deepest hopes and fears.

Journaling is also a powerful tool for accessing your intuition, the inner wisdom that's always at your fingertips. To gather information about a situation you're facing or a person you're dealing with, write down a specific question. Then immediately begin to write down the answer without thinking too much. That way, neither your logical mind nor your ego gets a chance to take over. To keep from focusing on a solution that you may want but that isn't in your best interest, pretend you're giving advice to someone else in your situation. With this technique, which is often called automatic writing, you're opening your intuitive "channel" to download information pertinent to your question, and it's coming from a fresh and unbiased perspective.

Over time, you'll discover just how powerful your words are. You'll be spending quality time with yourself and getting clarity on important issues in your life. You'll be able to observe the way you deal with sensitive issues. And the more you write about a particular subject, the more you'll be able to monitor your responses and see how you dealt with each situation. This is a tremendous help in creating a better blueprint for living your life.

SELF-INQUIRY: KNOWLEDGE FROM THE INSIDE OUT

How well are you balancing your active life with elements of calm reflection, introspection, and restoration? How deeply are you delving into the wisdom within you? Try asking yourself questions such as these:

- Am I continuing to learn and grow and to make my life better?

- Do people look to me for advice and counsel?

- Is it difficult for me to spend quiet time in reflection?

- Am I able to set aside part of my day for quiet time without distractions or outside influences?

- Do I feel anxious, edgy, or restless most of the time?

- Am I making the same mistakes again and again?

- Do I feel that my life is balanced between work and relaxation?

There is a solid connection between an intelligent mind and a peaceful mind; therefore, acquiring knowledge and a stronger sense of self improves not only your mind but also your spirit. Resting, meditation, and contemplation are excellent Yin activities. Taking a class, teaching, or acquiring a college degree would be formidable Yang pursuits. The balance of both energies strengthens your inner being. If you're constantly working on your to-do lists, it's a signal that you may *not* have a good balance between effort and contemplation in your life. If you need to write "time-out" on your to-do list in order to get it into your day, that's okay!

Career & Life Purpose

"Deep Water"

Core concepts: Courage, trust, depth, life purpose, life work

Personal practice: Listen to your inner voice and honor your soul's desire.

Soul qualities: Finding the path of least resistance, pursuing your passion, and surrendering to your inner guidance system

Vital lesson: Chase the inspiration, not the money.

Colors: Black, dark tones

Enhancements: Artwork depicting your career or images of water. Water features, mirrors, and glass items. Quotes relating to life purpose.

CHAPTER 12

WORKING YOUR CALLING

The Career and Life Purpose Gua

If we are facing in the right direction,
all we have to do is keep on walking.

— ANCIENT BUDDHIST PROVERB

Sometimes one room can change your life—and my clients Maggie and Kevin, a married couple in their 50s, proved it.

Maggie was a writer with a career as a professional speaker and life coach in the area of fitness and wellness. Kevin was an independent patent attorney specializing in digital data content authentication on the Internet. Both were successful but were looking to move their careers to the next level when they came to me for help.

"I've read lots of books on feng shui and felt totally confused," Maggie admitted. "Was our bed facing northwest, southeast . . . whatever? Did we have to knock out walls? Basically, I figured our home was a feng shui nightmare and gave up." Luckily, nothing is a lost cause in feng shui. Every room counts and every gua can be enhanced in ways that will change life, because everything is interconnected.

I went from room to room in Maggie and Kevin's house, not knocking down walls or buying all new furniture, but moving things around and repurposing what they already had. Everything from making their bedroom more about pairs to rearranging pieces in the living space to create a cozy environment for comfortable conversation and easy living. The goal was to simplify each room so that energy could flow freely and at full force.

When both members of a couple share the same goal—in this case, to boost their careers to the next level of financial and personal success—I focus on the energy in the entire space that relates to that goal. Both Maggie and Kevin worked from a shared home office, so when I stepped into that room, I knew I had come to the heart of the matter.

Their beige office was located in the Love, Marriage, and Relationships gua of the home, emphasizing how their separate careers were intertwined with their romantic partnership. In the room there were two desks, two tall bookcases, and a filing cabinet next to each of the desks. More filing cabinets still in their boxes were stacked in the middle of the room, unopened.

Though they had distinct careers, their offices were blended, therefore their energy was blended. Yet their desks were up against the walls on opposite sides of the room, so that they sat with their backs to each other. This was a very different problem from the one Shirley had faced—remember the client who couldn't work effectively in the office she shared with her boyfriend because his presence was a distraction and his energy sucked up all of hers? Here, the workstations facing the walls were blocking energy from moving across the desks, and by keeping their backs to each other, Maggie and Kevin were "turning away from their relationship" in order to focus on individual goals—okay for the goals, but not okay for a couple in a relationship.

First, I recommended they paint the back wall of the office red, to fire up the energy of their careers, their fame and reputation, and their love and marriage! The next step was to unpack the filing cabinets in the center of the room, which were clogging up the "hub of the wheel." We placed all the cabinets across the back red wall to create a solid foundation, as well as a central location for filing. Shared office equipment, such as the printer and fax machine, went on the top of the filing cabinets. Next we moved Kevin's desk from facing the wall to facing the "front" of the room—an open entryway from the kitchen, with no doors—in an L shape. I wanted him to have a commanding position. His bookcase of law reference books was placed on his side, in his "office." Now that he was no longer closed in or constrained by facing the wall, he immediately felt the difference.

Because the size of the room was limited, Maggie kept her desk facing the wall, yet we placed it where she had a clear view of the front of the room. Her bookcase was placed alongside her desk and filled with reference books on health and fitness. Diplomas, awards, and inspirational sayings were hung on each of the walls. On the rear red wall, artwork of a beach scene with two chairs facing in the same direction declares their unity and shared vision as partners. The water in the artwork represents career, since the water element corresponds to the Career gua.

In the Career and Life Purpose gua of their home, which included the approach to front door and entryway, I suggested that Maggie enhance the outside with a complete landscape makeover to boost her career possibilities. She not only completed a total transformation of vibrant plants and flowers, she added a water pond with koi fish. She repainted the entryway and hung a multifaceted energy crystal from the ceiling just beyond the front door meant to circulate prosperity entering by way of the front door throughout the home.

The new arrangement and clarity in their workspace combined with the enhancements to their Career and Life Purpose gua shifted things for them both in positive ways. Maggie decided to return to college for a degree in communications with an emphasis in English and writing; now, in addition to writing for various magazines, she authors a blog on fitness. Though Kevin had been skeptical of the feng shui approach at first—"no crystals or woo-woo," he told me—he too had to admit that it worked: he received a job offer from a large legal firm and is now a senior counsel directing the firm's efforts in electronic litigation. He also holds a prestigious position in the American Bar Association.

Today Maggie says she likes to call me the "Dr. Phil" of feng shui. "You did not come bearing smudge sticks or crystals," she wrote to me after our work was finished. "Instead, you came in like the Fire element, gangbusters. When we were finished, I could *feel* a different energy flow. We had guests that same evening and they said, 'We just love your home—it has such a nice feel to it.'"

WORKING WITH CAREER AND LIFE PURPOSE

Are you fulfilling your own destiny or following someone else's idea of what it ought to be? The Career and Life Purpose gua is the place to assess how well you're living up to your passion and your potential. Whether you're job-hunting, retired, working at something you love, or longing for a change, enhancements in this gua can help you stay purposefully connected to your path—especially when you're changing jobs, trying to use untapped skills, or questioning your purpose in life.

The Career and Life Purpose gua, located in the front middle third of the Bagua map—the front middle of a building, room, or surface—needs enhancements that reflect how you want to be living your life. To tailor the enhancements as specifically as possible to your desires, ask yourself, "What would my career look like if it were depicted in artwork?" The answer might be literal—an image of an airplane if you want to become a pilot, a symbol like the caduceus if you're in medicine—or it might be an abstraction that captures the essential energy of your dream. You can use this space to represent objectives at any point on your ideal path: if you want to retire to a waterfront villa, hang a print or photograph that shows such a scene in lush and loving detail. By now you understand visual energy, so you can see how these representations are effective enhancements to the energy of the space and powerful cues to you.

In many home layouts, this gua is an entryway—a highly suitable use, because the front door is considered the "mouth" of chi, and the fresh, active energy coming in keeps your purpose continuously renewed. If your floor plan gives you flexibility, this gua also makes a good library or family room, and of course it's highly effective as an office: any time you match a particular gua with a corresponding life function, such as Career and Life Purpose with a work space or Love, Marriage, and Relationships with a master bedroom, you're giving that life aspect an extra boost. What's more, because the front of the home is the site of active Yang energy, placing a working office there can help a home-based business bring in a steady stream of income. I once had two clients, real estate agents, who were married and working from home. Both of their offices were in the back, in the Yin area of the home. They had a very large living room in the front that they never used, so I asked them if they would consider moving their offices to this room just to try it out for a month. I suggested getting desks that were decorative from any perspective, with lots of plants and decorative screens to divide their spaces and create boundaries. Their only concern was noise from talking on the phone, but both agreed that when they were in their company's offices, they were in cubicles quite close to others, and the husband usually walked around with his cell phone during conversations anyway. They decided to give it a try, and their real estate business, which had been struggling in this challenging housing market, began to pick up speed.

As you know, I'm a proponent of using artwork and accessories with visual images that strongly convey the direction you are heading. Traditionally, Chinese households would place their most prized piece of artwork in the entryway to bring good luck and represent them as a family; my love of feng shui as a career, a lifestyle, and a template for managing my life is reflected in the artwork, furniture, and accessories in my own Career and Life Purpose gua entryway. One piece is jade shaped into a heart, mounted on gold silk, and framed. The other is an antique coin purse made of leather and adorned with jade pieces—the kind that wealthy men in China often wore hanging from the gold cords that tied their silk robes. My framed antique purse on gold silk represents wealth in the most traditional ways of the Chinese—the underpinnings of my feng shui calling—and anchors my wealth and prosperity in my career at the very entrance to my home.

The Water element, which is anchored in this gua, has energetic aspects that can also be incorporated into the décor. I use the color black to represent Water, in the form of a black lacquered piano-finish cabinet with traditional Chinese scenes in gold. Placed in the entryway, the cabinet holds my business brochures and supplies in its drawers.

THE WORK OF YOUR LIFE

Earlier in this book, we took a searching look at the idea of finding, honoring, and fulfilling your life's potential; ultimately, this is the goal of *all* feng shui. The Career and Life Purpose gua simply calls attention with special force to our authentic reason for being on this earth. While we can't escape the requirements of daily life, such as jobs, family obligations, and household chores, we still need to take time to explore a higher calling, and this gua can help us get down to the real work of our lives.

Most people can start by making a list: what they like to do or feel interested in versus what they don't like to do or have no interest in pursuing. Once you start doing an activity you enjoy, even in a small way—the way I began exploring feng shui while I was still working full time (and then some) at ESPN—you find out what comes easily to you. You don't have to be formally trained in a particular activity or subject, but you may find that further education will help you develop and perfect your skills. Sometimes a certification or degree provides the necessary credentials or credibility for a profession to blossom. In my case, my feng shui certification gives me professional legitimacy, something I find necessary because of the common perception that feng shui is more a hobby than a career path. The truth is, though, I instinctively and intuitively "get" feng shui, well beyond the formal training. It's natural to me—I was born to do it.

You might think that in today's world, with all those obligations weighing on you, this deep delving into authenticity would feel a lot like swimming upstream. In truth, though, I believe the way toward your purpose is ultimately the path of least resistance, because it's the one where your passion leads you. Your dreams of how you want to live your life should be vivid, accessible, and wildly exciting to you. Anything less is not living up to your soul's calling. Your livelihood is the natural outcome of letting your own ideas guide you: if you chase the inspiration, the money will soon follow.

Choosing to follow your true passion takes courage and trust, as you're often following intuitive prompts, trusting your instinct, and perhaps going in a direction that's out of your comfort zone in the short term. Trust, in turn, requires you to follow your passion one assignment at a time, in what may feel like baby steps, and to surrender the desire to control everything. It asks you to open yourself up to divine timing and intuitive guidance, which likewise appear in slow, insightful, and encouraging doses. And if you're unsure how to distinguish this guidance from your everyday thoughts, consider this piece of advice from author and teacher Doreen Virtue, Ph.D. She notes that when you think in the first person about what might happen if you follow your desires—*What if I fail?*—the ego is talking, and when you listen to the ego's message that you're flawed or bound for failure, your subconscious self starts working to make it so. On the other hand, when what pops into your head is in the second person—*You can do it*—you're tapping into deeper wisdom, and the ego is not getting in the way.

Trust—Learned and Earned

Not a day goes by that I don't remind myself to trust the process—to trust that while progress may be slow, strong will and determination will help me get to where I want to be. I think of trust as the steering mechanism by which we navigate life's journey. It works on several levels, starting with trusting yourself, believing that you have the ability to handle any situation life throws at you, knowing that you can learn from mistakes and gracefully move on.

Trust also means trusting others—when they earn our trust by matching their words and actions to commitments they've made, explicit or implicit. Even as you observe and evaluate, though, it's important to bring empathy and compassion to bear: accept that there are many sides to every story and that no one is perfect. Try not to let your ego undermine your trust in others: for example, don't succumb to suspicions that your partner is looking for someone better because you're not good enough. Your partner might very well be trustworthy, and constant doubting undermines a relationship.

As children, we learned to do what we were told even if our natural instincts told us otherwise. As adults, we have to learn trust in a new way, just as we learn any skill. While trust can be a feeling, it's also a conscious choice, and everyone is responsible for his or her own "trust competency." Build your own trustworthiness by taking responsibility for everything that happens in your life. If you overreact to a situation and undermine your self-worth, or if you complain to someone about someone else's behavior without first having an open and honest dialogue with that person, you can recognize a destructive pattern at work—not judging it, just discerning how it feeds or depletes your energy. If you can't accept your own imperfections, you can't expect others to do so.

Building trust with new friends or business associates is always challenging. Yet people with whom you have authentic relationships don't rebuff you when your behavior is less than stellar. Honest conversations without fear of disapproval or rejection are the key to building a strong connection. When you want to convey something that's bothering you, avoid teasing or sarcasm. Resist the temptation to drop hints about behavior you'd like to see change rather than talking openly about it. Have the courage to speak the truth without concern for the consequences.

Above all, have faith in a joyous future, even when you're facing uncertainty. Rely on the notion that people are generally good-hearted and life is full of abundance. You have opportunities to cultivate this kind of trust in every moment, because every choice you make in the course of a day has an impact on how you feel and where you will go in your life. Strive to let everything around you and everyone with whom you come in contact be consistent contributors of uplifting energy. Trust in your immeasurable potential to envision a bright and happy future—and then to *create* it.

SELF-INQUIRY: PURPOSE FROM THE INSIDE OUT

Are you on track with your life's work? Does the path you're taking serve your highest purpose? Explore these ideas with questions such as the ones below, or other questions you come up with that zero in on what's most relevant for you. Remember to keep the questions inwardly directed; instead of asking *How can I get a better job?* think along the lines of *Am I using my skills in the best way I can, for the highest good?*

- Is my job or career fulfilling to me?

- Am I passionate about the work I do?

- Do I take time to reflect on the reason I was placed on this earth?

- Does my life fulfill me spiritually as well as materially?

- Am I reaching my full potential?

- Do I trust other people readily?

- Do I trust my own inner guidance?

- Is there anything I feel I'm missing?

Let your answers guide you, gently, to new understanding of where you are and where you're headed.

Helpful People & Travel

"Creative Heaven"

Core concepts: Clarity, confidence, synchronicity, spirituality, patience, insight, maturity

Personal practice: Seek resonant spiritual guidance, helpers, teachers, mentors.

Soul qualities: Openness to the guidance of synchronicity

Vital lesson: You are always where you need to be.

Colors: White, grays, black

Enhancements: Figures representing spiritual beliefs or angels. Artwork and images of helpful people, mentors, or travel destinations. Display of spiritual quotes and affirmations.

CHAPTER 13

FINDING NEW DIRECTIONS

The Helpful People and Travel Gua

No matter what accomplishments you make, somebody helped you.

— ALTHEA GIBSON

When Shelley came to me, she was recently divorced and facing a common challenge—trying to sell a home—with an uncommon twist: the home was on an island in the Atlantic! It was a high-end property, and Shelley wanted to use the proceeds from the sale to temporarily relocate to the western area of the United States and ultimately be able to travel. Her dream was to be able to devote herself to raising her son, guiding and expanding his homeschool education while touring the world. Normally, that type of house in that location would have been an easy sale as a vacation home and investment property for an affluent family. But in this challenging real estate market, it was proving very difficult to move. "I'm in the wrong place at the wrong time," she lamented.

Though Shelley's situation involved an entire house, it was clear that her three challenges—making a difficult real estate sale, briefly relocating, and beginning her family's journey as world travelers—engaged one particular area of her *life*: the Helpful People and Travel gua.

She made the right call getting in touch with me. I could be her first helpful person! Shelley and I worked together by phone, using photos and the floor plan of her house. I gave information about how to stage her home, making a wonderful flow of energy, but what we really needed to focus on was the inner work that would strengthen her Helpful People and Travel gua.

My first step was to help her let go of her personal attachment to the home and her own decorating style. The essential tips I gave her to sell her home quickly and at fair market value included highlighting the home's strong points while minimizing the weak points by considering the arrangement of her furnishings through the buyers' eyes. While staging a home for sale involves many things, I wanted her motivation to be focused on transforming the dwelling into a comfortable and roomy environment, with a simple, elegant, and spacious presentation intended to invite prospective buyers to stay and linger.

The next step was to teach her the soul quality of synchronicity so the timing of the sale could follow a natural course and not be disrupted by her eagerness to move on. For her to realize her dream, she needed the perfect buyer (with cash or easily financed) to come in with the perfect price (asking price at fair market value) at the perfect time (coming together effortlessly). This required her to let go of control of the outcome and surrender to the process for the correct alignment to occur.

Shelley followed the simple staging advice I gave and worked with daily practices to bring more of the soul qualities of this gua into her daily life—and she sold the house for the asking price in less than two months. I also helped her select a new home with feng shui eyes. She wasn't in the wrong place at the wrong time after all. In feng shui terms, we never are.

WORKING WITH HELPFUL PEOPLE AND TRAVEL

The Helpful People and Travel gua is aimed at attracting what you need into your life—from clients to mentors to the inspiration of a higher connection. Helpful people come in many categories; they can include close friends, reliable family members, or a spiritual community that supports you during uncertain times. And don't underestimate the importance of having a network of helpers such as a good doctor, dentist, computer technician, therapist, or plumber!

This gua can also be used to amplify your chance to travel, whether you want to relocate to a new job or a new way of life—or simply enjoy leisure and adventure. As in the Career and Life Purpose gua, posters, artwork, or other objects that depict a destination you want to reach can help to focus energy in that direction. While I was working at ESPN, I wanted to pursue my dream of living in Florida and practicing feng shui full time. I knew I wanted a Mediterranean-style home adjacent to a body of water. So, while most ESPN executives' offices were decorated in sports memorabilia, I chose artwork that showed iconic scenes of Florida—palm trees and the like. I also hung a painting called *Toscana* of an iconic scene by a lake in Italy—buildings along the waterfront, classic Mediterranean forms, even boats in the water—with the precise colors I envisioned for my home. Within six months, I had found a house in a development in Florida, by a lake, with design and features strikingly similar to the painting in my office. The name of the home model was "Tuscany." That's how powerful feng shui can be in manifesting your desired outcome when your focus is strong and clear.

Not surprisingly, Helpful People and Travel is an ideal gua for a garage, the travel center of your home—and its location in the right front corner means it does wind up as a garage in the layout of many properties. It's also suitable for an office, living room, or family room; for an entryway, a natural function in the front of a home (though it shouldn't have a view of the kitchen or bathroom, as we've discussed, lest the prosperity coming in the door go symbolically down the drain); and possibly for a guest room, if traffic noise isn't a problem. To enhance this space, you may want to consider how you're perceived as a "helpful person": in your vocation, such as editor, nurse, or consultant, or as a spouse, friend, parent, or child. Then you can express the universal theme of helping others accordingly in the décor and function of the room.

In an office, for example, in order to be helpful to others, you need organization and clarity; tools and processes that help you do your job efficiently will serve your clients and customers. The goal is to create an atmosphere of service that attracts and retains clients who are naturally drawn to you. In a living room, you may want to create an atmosphere of closeness, comfort, and interaction. Often a formal living room is abandoned for the family room because its ambiance does not convey warmth or encourage conversation. In a Helpful People and Travel guest room, you can create a space of comfort, quiet, and fun for your guests. How might they need to supplement their wardrobes for things they're likely to do while staying with you? Can you supply a hat, sunglasses, beach towels, a spa robe? To make particular guests feel especially welcome, frame photos of them with you throughout the years and place them around the guest room. Their visit is creating lasting memories.

SURRENDERING TO SYNCHRONICITY

Synchronicity can be thought of as a sort of personal guidance system, leading us to those magical moments when we're drawn to respond to a clear need, or compelled to connect with a particular person, or inspired to take some action. Some call these happenings chance or mere coincidence; others see them as spiritual experiences. Either way, they can have a profound—even life-saving—impact. For whatever reason, paths intersect in a meaningful way, like a meeting at a crossroads. In daily life, an event or experience can connect you to an opportunity you hadn't considered before. If you get a phone call from someone you were just thinking about but haven't spoken to in ages, that's a moment of synchronicity, too.

Clarity and confidence, insight and patience, intention and the law of attraction all come into play in the Helpful People and Travel gua, whereby you are called upon to allow yourself to be introduced to new people, situations, and ways of doing things through unplanned connections that open unexpected doors. This is the essence of synchronicity. You are surrendering to what you can't control and allowing the hectic flow and rhythm of your pursuits to relax.

If we think of synchronous events as messages, we're able to look at our lives in a new way. We can go from taking the predictable path to following a new, inspired one. If a perfectly timed "meeting of the ways" comes to you, all you have to do is cooperate—by keeping an open mind, having the strength and courage to follow your heart, and surrendering to the subtle nudge to explore something you might not have pursued otherwise. In our fast-paced world, we often feel that we have to set lofty goals and multitask aggressively if we're to accomplish anything at all, let alone manifest our dreams. Instead of chasing your goals at every moment, see how much you can let your day unwind organically. Put your to-do list aside, even for a day, and let synchronicity set the pace.

To activate synchronicity, clear your schedule and indulge in some activity you enjoy that gets you out into the community, such as a craft fair, a farmers' market, or a walk on the beach. Leave ordinary problems for another day and just enjoy the rhythms of life. Stroll down an uncharted path and see what happens.

Your Magical Day

The lesson of the Helpful People and Travel gua is simple and reassuring: *you are always where you need to be.* However, that doesn't mean you shouldn't spend time thinking about where you *want* to be! I'll share with you one of my favorite exercises for envisioning how you want to live your life by creating one magical day. This isn't the same as chasing your goals and not letting things unfold—it's a way of laying a foundation that your life can unfold *from,* one magical day at a time. You have to build your ideal life day by day in order to know who or where you need to go to find the teachers, mentors, and inspiration to support your dream.

I look at creating your "magical day" scenario as creating a framework, defining your vision. Synchronicity is what connects the dots to fill it in. Remember, in feng shui you're always using complementary tools to create balance and harmony. Framing your magical day is structure (Yang), and synchronicity is the unchained, loose movement within that framework (Yin). Though they may sound contradictory, both are needed to create balance. Gradually, you'll see that more and more of your actual day will align with your vision, and from there you'll move to a magical week, month, year, and so on. As an added benefit, mapping out your ideal day will let you see where you need to attract helpful people to support you in making it a reality!

Designing your magical day begins in your imagination. You're creating a vision of all that is possible, so take a moment to abandon any potential roadblocks, such as insufficient funds, lack of training or education, or simple fear. You embody distinct talents and vast potential ready to be expressed; if you get caught up in the notion that other people have ideas similar to yours, only better, you risk deflating your own desire to try. Don't assume that being "original" means doing something that's never been done before—that's like saying there can be only one Picasso, so why bother to paint? The 12 notes in a musical scale can be rearranged time and again to produce an infinite number of original melodies. In the same way, your ideas will come together in a way that's different from anyone else's.

Holding in mind the essence of what makes you unique, now let yourself dream of what your ideal day would look and feel like from morning to night. It may not bear any resemblance to your real life—your imagination has no boundaries—but then again, it may.

- Do you wake up to an alarm or sleep till you wake up naturally?

- Do you take 20 minutes for quiet reflection with a cup of tea, or read the morning paper, or both?

- If you work for a living, what is your job or career? What kind of work exactly do you do?

- Is your job full time or part time? How many hours do you work each week?

- When you come home at the end of the day, who's there to greet you? A partner? A pet? Both?

- In the evening, do you socialize with friends, immerse yourself in a creative project, or retreat with a good book?

- How do you spend your other leisure time?

- Do you volunteer in the community?

- How do you maintain a healthy lifestyle?

When I left my corporate career to start my own business, I had the perfect opportunity to dream up my own magical day—and the freedom to do as much as possible to match it. It was a chance to reinvent my life, blending work and play in just the right proportions. It was a fresh start, with no preconceived ideas, structure, or rules that I had to follow. At the beginning, I didn't focus on business models or long-term goals. I wanted to create one model day that was interesting, exciting, fulfilling, and joyful, then use it as a building block for the weeks, months, and years ahead.

So I sat quietly and thought through every part of the day. I imagined what my home would look like (that's where *Toscana* came in), what kinds of relationships I would develop, and ways I could lead an inspiration-driven life every day. Here's what it looked like.

Each morning my beloved and I wake up without an alarm to the light of the expanding sunrise. I feel rested and optimistic about how the day will unfold. The first thing I do is open the door to the room where our kitty sleeps and let her out onto the screened lanai—she enjoys our sunny Sarasota mornings as much as we do.

We brew our favorite coffee or tea and curl up in chairs on the lanai to take in the stillness and quiet beauty of the lake view and the graceful movement of the tropical birds. Soon the fountains will turn on and send out their spherical ripples. I lounge with my laptop, checking e-mail and the morning news. Once I've reconnected with the world, I retreat for 30 private minutes of meditation and journaling.

In a leisurely way, we prepare and eat our healthy breakfast, chatting about the day's activities. We may take a walk or go for a bike ride. Soon after, I call my parents for our daily chat in between visits. I let them know they are loved and appreciated, so that each day I'm banking wonderful memories of my family.

I'm keen on beginning my workday no earlier than 10 A.M., whether it be with a feng shui consultation, a speaking engagement, watercolor painting, new product or project development, marketing, a volunteer venture, or writing. As much as possible, I keep Mondays open to ensure an extended and rejuvenating weekend. I also use Mondays to plan the month ahead. I create slots in my schedule to plug in appointments, business and social engagements, and prep time so I'm able to pace myself. While each day is different, I try to conclude my work by 5 P.M.

Evenings are mostly reserved for social activities, relaxation, and fun. We love to entertain family and friends at home, as we dabble in preparing organic gourmet cuisine! We also enjoy evenings out, which may include fine dining, dancing, a movie, or a sunset cruise. We've both had our fair share of business travel, so leisure travel always has a spiritual component, with a destination that nurtures a sense of wonder and adventure.

Before I go to bed, I express my gratitude for all that's been given to me.

Now it's your turn. In a journal or notebook, write a story in the present tense about your magical day. Write it as if it were happening this very day. If you like, you can use my version as a template to create your own. Include any occupation, event, relationship, or experience essential to your happiness. Dream big, as if you had a magic wand you could wave to create exactly what you want. It doesn't matter if it all feels like pure fantasy or if it seems quite out of your reach. Just make it up—just pretend. When you're done, it may surprise you to discover that, with some simple adjustments, you can begin to enjoy some aspects of your vision right now. After all, why postpone happiness?

The objective is to integrate as many pieces of your magical day as possible into your reality. For example, if you have to be at a job by 9 A.M., could you compress your idyllic morning routine into some time frame before 8:30? If so, you may have to set an alarm clock or, if you prefer to wake up naturally, go to bed earlier. If you have limited control over your day because of family or work obligations, allocate just a small amount of time to exploring areas you'd like to expand. If you want to paint, make time to paint, either on your own at home or by taking a class. If having a relationship or being married is important, yet missing from your life, continue to live your life while making room to invite in a loving relationship, perhaps by pursuing new activities where you're likely to meet like-minded people.

The more you can organize parts of your actual day to align with your ideal one, the more you'll feel a sense of satisfaction and contentment unfolding. You'll feel hopeful, and that will give you momentum to persevere until all 24 hours of the day are designed to your complete satisfaction.

The next step is to create an action plan to make those 24 hours more and more possible. Would that require additional experience, money, or education? Might it mean going back to school, getting technical training, or becoming an intern or a volunteer? Is there someone who inspires you? If so, ask for a 20-minute information-gathering interview to find out what steps he or she had to take to achieve success. The point is: never feel you're stuck with what you're doing right now. Your life is not a life sentence. Creating your magical day helps to lay the foundation for a new way of life and open a channel for synchronicity and support to flow in. If you start now, without reservations, you'll be healthier, happier, and a lot more fun to be around.

Self-Inquiry: Support from the Inside Out

How deep does your support system go—both visible and invisible? Are you drawing on spiritual as well as practical help for the life you want to live? Use these questions, or others of your own choosing, to explore the role of support and synchronicity in your life.

- Do I have a reliable group of friends and family members?

- Are the people close to me supportive of my hopes and dreams?

- Do I want to feel more spiritually connected?

- Do I constantly feel the weight of the world on my shoulders?

- Do I feel as if every minute of the day is taken up, without a break?

- Do I want to travel more, for work or for pleasure?

- Are there tasks or challenges in my life that I feel I can't manage on my own?

- Am I able to leave my to-do list behind and just enjoy the day's events as they unfold?

Your answers to these questions may help you see where you could use some support and inspiration—and perhaps start giving you some ideas about where to seek out the help you need.

Earth

"Center"

Core concepts: Balance, groundedness, unity, calm, connectedness, self-awareness, completion, harmony, enlightenment

Personal practice: Be conscious, present, and aware.

Soul qualities: Tuning in to your inner voice and harmonizing with your inner truth

Vital lesson: Love what is.

Colors: Yellows, earth tones

Enhancements: Artwork and objects of peaceful images. Items that come from the earth or nature.

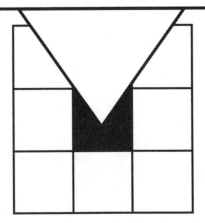

CHAPTER 14

CALM AT THE CENTER

The Earth Gua

Learn to drink the cup of life as it comes.
— AGNES TURNBULL

I've talked a lot in this book about how feng shui wisdom calls on us to be present in the moment—to accept what is right now, no matter how difficult—and to understand that every situation can be transformed into a blessing. When we approach it with this awareness, the moment, like the Earth center of a home, becomes a still point of perfect peace. And even though I'm a professional feng shui practitioner and teacher, this is a lesson I've needed to have taught to me as well. The epitome of Earth is being able to relax within the flow of life. We continue to receive information without clouding it with expectations or fear. Whenever we are pushed or pulled out of our center, we graciously return to a balanced state by accepting responsibility for our decisions and actions.

In feng shui, animals represent the Fire element, bringing good energy into our environment as we experience the endless pleasure of their company. They also serve as our teachers, leading us on a journey of self-discovery that we would have never experienced without them. They are the guardians of soul wisdom, as they use their senses quite differently than we do. Their communication often comes by way of rubbing against us, using their paws to touch us, and having a natural curiosity about everything *we* do.

Six and a half years ago, I stepped into an animal rescue shelter to adopt a kitten. I have always had female cats, so I surprised myself by choosing a male kitten who just wouldn't let me leave without him. I promptly named him Sydney. This would be the first of many lessons: to go where you have never been, you have to do what you have never done. Sydney was no ordinary pet. Lively and precocious at first, after three months, Sydney stopped playing with his toys and started sitting quietly off to the side. I noticed that he would clumsily bump into things, as if he had no idea what was directly in front of him. After some simple testing using a cotton ball (it has no smell or sound), the vet discovered that Sydney was totally blind.

The vet told me that some people who find out their pets are blind elect to give them up or put them to sleep. But I felt that I was somehow divinely selected to care for Sydney, and I felt honored. People who met him didn't always know he was blind, as all of his other senses were heightened, including his intuition. As a special needs kitty, he actually became influential in my feng shui practice by teaching me how to create and maintain an ideal living environment, free of clutter. When you get home at the end of a workday and flop your briefcase on the floor just inside the door, you are instantly reminded that this becomes an unforeseen obstacle for a cat who can't see! In feng shui, every object must have a home, and cluttered pathways block essential energy from moving freely in the environment. Sydney became the gentle reminder to honor my sacred space.

The condition that caused Sydney's blindness eventually leads to additional health challenges, including chronic kidney disease. This is an old cat's condition in a very young cat, and it requires ongoing medical treatment with essential fluids to flush out toxins. I learned how to administer the fluids to Sydney via daily injections. Every time I started to worry that I might not be able to afford his treatments, I was blessed with an abundance of calls for feng shui consultations. The more I gave my care and affection to Sydney, the more I learned that the Universe would never deny me the ability to care for him.

I knew that this condition might shorten Sydney's life, and sometimes it was hard to stay in the moment and keep the sadness of that knowledge away. Sydney helped me here too. This cat loved life so much that his blindness and illness never kept him from living to his full potential and receiving abundant affection from all who came into his presence. Just the simple act of sitting in the lanai and feeling the soft breeze was a joy for him. No one felt sorry for him because he didn't feel sorry for himself.

To ensure that Sydney would have an abundance of healing care beyond his physical care, I decided to become a Reiki master. By learning to transmit energy to his body through touch, I was able to give him comfort, shift blockages, and stimulate physical healing, and I believe that this helped Sydney overcome a series of serious health challenges. He loved how the Reiki energy soothed his body and improved the quality of his life, while at the same time it connected the two of us on a much deeper level.

While I was visiting my parents in California over the Christmas holidays, Sydney became very ill and was taken to the veterinary clinic for critical care. Sydney had decided it was his time—but he waited for me to return home so we could have some time together before his passing. His greatest lesson was teaching me to love deeply without fear, as there was nothing I wouldn't do for this caring and special companion. I knew that his spirit would continue to be with me in all that I did. After all, Sydney always lived in the present moment!

Your Life in Balance

Life circles around the Earth center of your home like a wheel around its hub. Located in the middle third of the middle row of the Bagua map, this is your home's pivot point, where all the other guas meet. When you attend to all these aspects of your life on a regular basis, you bring them into harmony, which is a position of power: like neutral gear on a car, it holds the potential for you to move forward or backward according to the needs of the moment. This position is the foundation for reaching your *own* full potential, because when all the aspects of your life are manageable, you feel safer, more secure, and freer to focus on your life work with clarity and purpose.

Earth is also the point of perfect balance—between Yin and Yang, among the Five Elements, and among all the facets of your life: work and play, self-image and outer image, family relationships and romantic bonds. In your daily life, you can create harmony within each of these facets, for example, in a particular relationship or even a single conversation. By working on all the guas, you can also create balance across all the energetic qualities of your life, which strengthens your center. We try all sorts of things to get centered—going to yoga class, taking a walk in nature, setting aside time for prayer—and though these activities are precious if they nourish our spirits, when you bring your life into balance, you find your center effortlessly. You might say it finds you! At the same time, by enhancing the Earth center of your home, you can help yourself feel both more energized and more grounded in every area. In a real sense, the Earth gua brings together all the work you've done throughout this book, because the underlying principle of feng shui *is* balance. Its goal is a whole life lived in harmony, grounded in what is essential and true.

It's also a life lived essentially in the present moment. In my own life, I use two reminders to keep me present, not projecting too far into the future or fixating on the past, good or bad. One is Sydney and the other is my mother. I mentioned earlier in the book that my mom has Alzheimer's disease and has lost much of her short-term memory. When I'm visiting my parents, we'll go to breakfast, and if the meal is bad, my dad will complain about it all day long. It wasn't served hot, it was too much money for too little food, and on and on. And my mom will say, "We had breakfast?" It always makes me laugh—and jump right back into the present moment.

Why complain about something in your past? It connects you to a negative story, and the story is told over and over. Being in the present moment, though, takes conscious effort and a lot of practice. If something is going on that is challenging and therefore on my mind, I constantly say to myself, "This too shall pass." It reframes the moment and reminds me it's just an uncomfortable moment. I even wear a thumb ring that is engraved with the phrase "This too shall pass." It's my visual reminder. So I keep photos of Sydney and my mom as visual reminders too, and I thank them every evening for the lesson on being in the now.

When I was in the jungle in Ecuador, one of my fellow travelers said, "This is the first time in my life that I have been somewhere where every moment is amazing." That was the perfect description. It was impossible for me to think about anything else while in the jungle. Back at home in Sarasota, with bills, obligations, and reminders of my "real" life all around me, I have to work harder to keep in the present moment, so I literally ask myself the question *What is going on right now that is amazing?* I can always find an answer.

Working with Earth

Traditionally, in China, the center of a home was likely to be an atrium or a courtyard—free of heavy objects, aligned with the natural surroundings, an open energy center for the household. It was the hub of the wheel, and it became a model for keeping the center of each room unblocked as well. In fact, the islands in the middle of so many modern Western kitchens, in feng shui terms, actually create blockages at the heart of the room's energy. In the United States today, the center of a home might be a room, a hallway (as in a center-hall Colonial), a staircase, or a space where several rooms open into one another.

You can enhance the Earth gua with any object or art piece that reflects peaceful surroundings, or any item that connects you to nature. This might mean crystals, plants, earthenware, shells, or pinecones; it might mean artwork with serene images or landscapes. You may also want to invoke images and materials that ground you by expressing the essence of who you are. In the home of a writer, for example, the Earth center might be anchored by shelves full of books, with the extra earthy component of natural materials (paper, binding). However you decorate it, it's important to keep the Earth center uncluttered and spacious in order for the vital energy to expand outward to the surrounding guas. Walk each of the pathways into, out of, and through the room: can you move freely? If your path is blocked, try to shift the arrangement of the furniture to create a freer flow.

To access the inner wisdom of Earth, simply turn within yourself to cultivate the essential qualities of the Earth gua: harmony, connection, awareness, and, crucially, gratitude. In this calm, clear space, life asks you simply to be present and love what is. Gratitude is key to inviting more good fortune and prosperity into your life. And what better way to express your gratitude than to simply say, "Thank you"?

CHANGING THE WORLD TWO WORDS AT A TIME

It seems as if people are frustrated about everything these days and can't wait to share their story with you. Whether it's the state of the economy, concerns about health and health care, or the fears and frustrations of the job market, people want to complain. You rarely see positive stories on the evening news, and when they do appear, they have to include an adorable animal to arouse a snippet of compassion.

To accept life just as it is, the downs as well as the ups, is to understand what the feng shui philosophy is all about. The ebb and flow of life is Yin and Yang in action, Nature's way of balancing the extremes. The housing market is a prime example of bringing order to extreme chaos: for many years the booming real estate market was fueled by greed rather than by a genuine increase in the intrinsic value of our homes. Ultimately, something had to restore balance, and so the industry, having spiraled out of control, finally spiraled downward. Once you accept that this is part of the natural cycle of life, you don't get caught up in your own expectations of how life should conduct itself.

As a self-proclaimed perfectionist, I spent a good portion of my life trying to create near-perfect conditions by controlling my career, my relationships, and my appearance. Instead of being content with and thankful for what I already had, I thought I always had to strive for something better. My attachment to perfection fueled my competitive spirit, and I felt I had to collect certain things and maintain a certain look in order to seem accomplished and appealing.

Feng shui has helped me design a way of living that is kinder, calmer, more compassionate, and more evenly paced—in part by letting go of my expectations of perfection and developing an attitude of gratitude for things as they are. While I was always pretty good at saying thank you when someone gave me a gift or did something nice for me, I wasn't often aware of all the other blessings around me that provided opportunities to be grateful. (I even had a hard time accepting compliments and would usually dismiss them by pointing out one of my imperfections.) In order to change this pattern, I decided to make a habit of saying thank you from the moment I got up until the moment I went to bed. Now, having a blissful night of sleep, rising to a sunny (or rainy) day, enjoying my work, having loving family and friends, and having enough money to pay my bills just scratches the surface of all the things I'm grateful for. I say thank you out loud at every opportunity. And the more I make a routine of this, the more I become aware of how many things are really going well for me.

When you enhance all the other guas, you are creating harmony and peace and a sense of being "centered," which is the essence of the Earth gua. When you are feeling easy and calm, it's easier to be aware of and grateful for every blessing in your life. I think at first you have to practice appreciation and gratitude just as you would begin exercise to build your muscles. Once you have some muscle tone, you don't think so much about it; you just continue to develop the muscle.

One way to structure a gratitude practice is to use the Bagua map itself as a focus for a simple meditation, acknowledging the many blessings that you already enjoy in each gua. It shifts your focus to what's positive, and you may find it lifts your spirits powerfully. Here's how this meditation might look for me:

- **Wealth and Prosperity:** *I'm grateful that all I truly need is provided and that I'm able to earn a living doing what I love the most. I'm conscious that giving my time, talent, or money to others who are less fortunate than I am is the greatest way to show my gratitude for all I have.*

- **Fame and Reputation:** *I'm aware that my lasting legacy is to treat myself and others with respect, compassion, and understanding, and that my charity work and contributions help make a difference in people's lives.*

- **Love, Marriage, and Relationships:** *I'm mindful to love myself as I am and to be kind and loving to all living things that inhabit the earth. I make time daily to tell my loved ones how much I care about them.*

- **Health and Family:** *I'm thankful for being guided to the most qualified health practitioners for myself and for my family. I'm learning to look after not only my physical health, but my mental, emotional, and spiritual health as well.*

- **Creativity and Children:** *I'm aware that I have been blessed with original ideas and artistic talents that are uniquely my own. I'm also reminded that every day I can make room for fun, laughter, and playtime that calms and soothes my soul.*

- **Knowledge and Self-Cultivation:** *I'm fortunate to be able to find books, teachers, and mentors available to help me grow and evolve into a kinder and more compassionate person. I now take time out of my day and give myself permission to relax, meditate, take a nap, or just be, without guilt.*

- **Career and Life Purpose:** *I'm thankful for the opportunity to become a feng shui consultant, teacher, and writer. I am clear that it is my passion, and I enjoy helping others discover their full potential this way.*

- **Helpful People and Travel:** *I'm grateful for the spiritual guidance I trust that I receive, along with support from friends, family, and mentors, to carefully guide me on my journey.*

- **Earth:** *When I am conscious and present to all that is available in the abundant Universe, I'm able to feel calm, grounded, and peaceful.*

You can do this all day, every day, with or without a formal framework. When you're able to start your car on the first try, say thank you. You're acknowledging that it's working properly and you're able to get on your way. When you charge through a yellow light at an intersection and get a ticket, say thank you: you're being reminded to slow your pace to keep yourself and others safe. Envision everyone in the world becoming more relaxed and peaceful in that safety.

Saying thank you—and saying it often—trains you to respond differently to the dramas of life. By pushing away critical viewpoints, you're automatically developing compassion, understanding, and empathy. Sincerely and graciously accept every compliment you receive. Be grateful for everyone who believes in you, cares about you, supports you, helps you, understands you, and trusts you. Even the electric company trusts you when providing service to your home—they trust that you have the ability and the intention to pay. Say thank you when you turn your lights on! If we each do our part, we can change the world two words at a time.

Self-Inquiry: Centering from the Inside Out

How calm is your center? Where do you need more peace? Ask yourself the questions below, or questions you devise yourself, to assess how well you're grounded in your life.

- Do I feel that my work and my personal life are in balance?

- Are my physical, emotional, mental, and spiritual states of health all supporting one another?

- Can I easily make decisions—even difficult ones—with clarity and purpose?

- Am I able to be in the present moment?

- Do I often feel anxious or distressed?

- Would I describe my life as peaceful?

- Am I happy most of the time?

If your answers point to feeling more pressure than peace, try to put yourself in situations that encourage more peaceful feelings. If peace is hard to come by, go back and review each of the guas and try to determine which life aspect you're feeling discontented with. That's what requires your attention right now to get to the peaceful present moment.

LAST WORD

Peace.
It does not mean to be
in a place where there is no noise,
trouble or hard work.
It means to be in the midst of those things
and still be calm in your heart.

— UNKNOWN

The truth is that there's no such thing as a "last word" in feng shui. The work is never completed—you'll never be "feng shui'ed." In the world around us and within us, things are always evolving—night turns to day, the seasons change, we get older. Life is constant change, and feng shui is a method for working with change.

In the course of this book, I hope you've learned to quiet your mind and open a calm, bright space for a sense of your true self to emerge. Maybe you've identified steps you want to take to bring yourself closer to your full potential in one particular area of life or across the board. To go forward with the work you've started, keep revisiting all the aspects of the Bagua map to see where harmony prevails and where adjustments are called for. You can do this in whatever way works for you. I like to go around the map clockwise and check in with each life aspect on a daily or weekly basis. If all is going well in a particular area, I don't make any changes within or without. Where things feel out of balance, I look for ways to restore it, either by adjusting something in my physical space or by inquiring more deeply into my inner life.

There isn't a week that goes by that there isn't some sort of test. For me, it might be as simple as dealing with an allergy of my pet's that needs attention or trying to come up with a new idea for a watercolor painting. Or it could be something more demanding, such as the health of my parents. These calls to action are gifts and opportunities, and I use the feng shui tools to achieve my highest good.

The most difficult challenge for me every day is to stay in the present moment, where my true source of power and potential resides. If I'm engaging in gossip, annoyed at another person's behavior, or playing the role of a victim, I know I'm wedged in the past. If my daydreaming and wishful thinking turn into wondering, worrying, or anxiety, I know I am dwelling on the outcome of an unknown future. These feelings are indicators, locators of who I am at any moment in time. Life's blessings, though, are found in the now, and buds of good fortune come to flower with exposure to appreciation, attention, and affection . . . for all that you have and all that you have to give.

WITH GRATITUDE

Writing can be a very soulful and lonely process. I am deeply grateful to so many whose knowledge, influence, and inspiration made this book possible.

The very first life-changing book I read was *You Can Heal Your Life* by Louise Hay. It's an essential reference book on my iPad and a continuous source of inspiration. Louise Hay and Reid Tracy opened the door and welcomed me into Hay House, fulfilling a lifelong dream of mine.

Many thanks to Laura Gray, Hay House acquisitions editor, for her careful reading and invaluable detailed suggestions for the manuscript, and for cheerfully guiding me through every step of the publishing process.

I so appreciate the razor-sharp vision, industry expertise, and personal support of Hay House director of acquisitions Patty Gift for believing in this project.

Anne Barthel is a brilliant editor with the innate ability to strengthen my words without changing my ideas and to help me express abstract ideas genuinely. I am forever grateful for her superb ability to structure the book, create a rhythmical flow, and cultivate my vision.

I thank Hadley Fitzgerald, a feng shui expert and mentor, who helped me in the early stages with expanding the content and gave me straightforward feedback while at the same time building my confidence.

To my gifted literary agent, Cynthia Cannell, for her unwavering belief in me combined with her tireless efforts, savvy business sense, invaluable feedback, and friendship. She saw potential in me from the very beginning and is the champion of my work.

To Peggy Rometo, my soul sister, I'm forever grateful to you for opening all the magical doors, fostering my instinctive intuitive ability, introducing me to Cynthia Cannell—and for lighting my pathway into the doors of Hay House. Your certainty and generosity shaped the spirit and quality of my feng shui endeavors.

To Jack Hyman, my soul brother and talented writer, for your rich friendship, moral support, and steadfast belief that I can do anything. I can't imagine living life to its fullest without you.

For my family of friends Connie (Wahine) Black, Sandy (Honah) Morimoto, Joanne (Josie) Giannini, and Maria Green, I'm so lucky to live in your love. Your enthusiasm and encouragement every step of the way fueled my ability to write.

For my support team, Connie Belmont, Mare Petras and Steve Teppler, Carol Snyder Gannon, Tracie Martin, Barbara Parker, Antoinette Fiumos, and Susan Polakoff Shaw, thank you for your treasured friendship.

With Gratitude

Many thanks to my master teacher, Terah Kathryn Collins, and the Western School of Feng Shui, for the essential contribution they have made to the discipline of feng shui and for introducing me to feng shui as a way of living my life to its fullest. My dedicated feng shui teachers and mentors, Becky Iott, Karen Carrasco, and Liv Kellgren, for their timeless knowledge and inspiration.

Karen Kingston, whose book *Clear Your Clutter with Feng Shui* forever changed my career path, thank you for helping me simplify my life.

To my mom and dad, Elsie and Gilbert George, for their profound influence, sacrifices, support, and encouragement to be my true self. I love you.

And to my clients and students who shared their stories, honored me with their trust, and invited me into their homes, thank you. Your personal feng shui success stories continually energize my passion for feng shui. Together we can change the world, one room at a time.

ABOUT THE AUTHOR

Cheryl Grace is a feng shui author, professional consultant, motivational speaker, and teacher who specializes in helping people design their lives from the inside out. As an expert practitioner, she offers a new perspective, putting the true power of feng shui in her readers' hands so they can reach their full potential by living an inspired and purpose-driven life.

With her illuminating insight and refreshing humor, she is a sought-after feng shui design professional and keynote speaker, turning the ancient wisdom of feng shui into a uniquely powerful program of discovery and self-fulfillment. Through the lens of feng shui, she decoratively transforms a home or business into a cozy and easy environment with an emphasis on modern decorating solutions that are practical as well as purposeful.

Grace is president and CEO of Redecorating . . . with feng shui, the highly regarded consultancy based in Sarasota, Florida, that she founded after a successful career as a corporate executive at ESPN. She graduated from Fresno State University and earned a master's degree from the University of San Francisco. As a watercolor artist, she has a line of Living Art® home décor and artwork inspired by feng shui available on her website, www.CherylGrace.com.

FENG SHUI DESIGN RESOURCES

PROFESSIONAL CONSULTATION SERVICES FOR RESIDENTIAL, BUSINESS, OR STAGING

An in-home or office feng shui consultation can produce many positive and inspiring results. Anytime you want to increase prosperity and remove obstacles that stand in your way, a feng shui consultation clears a path for personal growth and new opportunities.

Cheryl Grace, president and creative director of Redecorating . . . with feng shui, offers expert refinement of your home by arranging your favorite things in a creative new way, using key design values of texture, shape, scale, and color. Your personal taste and unique style are encouraged throughout the consultation.

Cheryl provides expert planning and arrangement of offices and employee stations for creative and productive business environments. By using her exclusive professional staging service, you can turn your home or business into instant ReSale potential without investing in expensive remodeling, design fees, or new furniture.

"When Cheryl came into my home and demonstrated ways to arrange my furniture to form a more flowing and pleasing environment, I was not just convinced, I became a convert! Her knowledge of feng shui and interior refinement has made my home less cluttered, more interesting, and has enhanced personal areas of my life that were both unexpected as well as life affirming! She had an uncanny ability to focus on what worked for my particular space and lifestyle!" Jack Hyman, writer, New York City

FENG SHUI HOME DÉCOR AND ENERGY ENHANCEMENTS

Living Art® feng shui décor and energy enhancements, designed by feng shui practitioner and watercolor artist Cheryl Grace, are available to enrich and accent your home or office. Each piece of art, jewelry, and energy enhancement is handmade with only the finest-quality materials and is inspired by the essential and beneficial elements of good feng shui.

As a Reiki master, Cheryl infuses each item with healing energy. They are truly one-of-a-kind creations that also make wonderful gift ideas for birthdays, anniversaries, awards, corporate gifts, and any special occasion or holiday celebration.

For more information on feng shui consultations by Cheryl Grace and Living Art® décor, visit **www.CherylGrace.com.**

Hay House Titles of Related Interest

All of the above are available at your local bookstore,
or may be ordered by contacting Hay House (see next page).

We hope you enjoyed this Hay House Insights
book. If you'd like to receive our online catalog
featuring additional information on Hay House books
and products, or if you'd like to find out more
about the Hay Foundation, please contact:

INSIGHTS

Hay House, Inc., P.O. Box 5100, Carlsbad, CA 92018-5100
(760) 431-7695 or (800) 654-5126
(760) 431-6948 (fax) or (800) 650-5115 (fax)
www.hayhouse.com® • **www.hayfoundation.org**

·Ọ·

Published and distributed in Australia by:
Hay House Australia Pty. Ltd., 18/36 Ralph St., Alexandria NSW
2015 • *Phone: 612-9669-4299* • *Fax: 612-9669-4144*
www.hayhouse.com.au

Published and distributed in the United Kingdom by:
Hay House UK, Ltd., Astley House,
33 Notting Hill Gate, London W11 3JQ
Phone: 44-20-3675-2450 • *Fax: 44-20-3675-2451*
www.hayhouse.co.uk

Published and distributed in the Republic of South Africa by: Hay
House SA (Pty), Ltd., P.O. Box 990, Witkoppen 2068
Phone/Fax: 27-11-467-8904 • www.hayhouse.co.za

Published in India by: Hay House Publishers India, Muskaan
Complex, Plot No. 3, B-2, Vasant Kunj, New Delhi 110 070
Phone: 91-11-4176-1620 • *Fax: 91-11-4176-1630*
www.hayhouse.co.in

Distributed in Canada by: Raincoast, 9050 Shaughnessy St.,
Vancouver, B.C. V6P 6E5 • *Phone: (604) 323-7100*
Fax: (604) 323-2600 • www.raincoast.com

·Ọ·

Take Your Soul on a Vacation

Visit **www.HealYourLife.com®** to regroup, recharge, and
reconnect with your own magnificence.
Featuring blogs, mind-body-spirit news, and life-changing
wisdom from Louise Hay and friends.

Visit **www.HealYourLife.com** today!